D0104428

formatio
TRADITION. EXPERIENCE.
TRANSFORMATION.

Formatio books from InterVarsity Press follow the rich tradition of the church in the journey of spiritual formation. These books are not merely about being informed, but about being transformed by Christ and conformed to his image. Formatio stands in InterVarsity Press's evangelical publishing tradition by integrating God's Word with spiritual practice and by prompting readers to move from inward change to outward witness. InterVarsity Press uses the chambered nautilus for Formatio, a symbol of spiritual formation because of its continual spiral journey outward as it moves from its center. We believe that each of us is made with a deep desire to be in God's presence. Formatio books help us to fulfill our deepest desires and to become our true selves in light of God's grace.

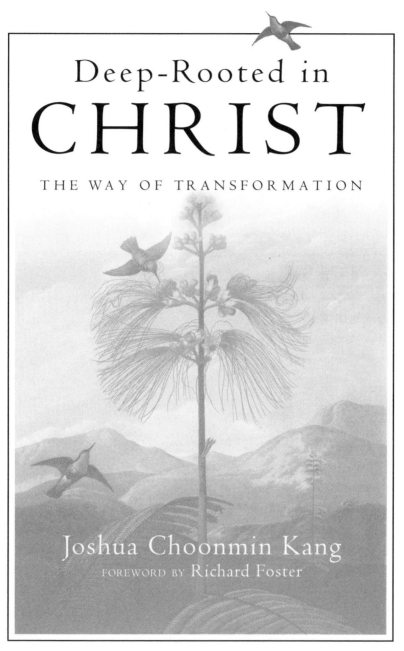

Deep-Rooted in
CHRIST

THE WAY OF TRANSFORMATION

Joshua Choonmin Kang

FOREWORD BY Richard Foster

IVP Books

An imprint of InterVarsity Press
Downers Grove, Illinois

The author is donating his royalties to World Vision.

InterVarsity Press
P.O. Box 1400, Downers Grove, IL 60515-1426
World Wide Web: www.ivpress.com
E-mail: mail@ivpress.com

Korean original ©2006 by Joshua Choonmin Kang

English translation ©2007 by Joshua Choonmin Kang

All rights reserved. No part of this book may be reproduced in any form without written permission from InterVarsity Press.

InterVarsity Press® is the book-publishing division of InterVarsity Christian Fellowship/USA®, a student movement active on campus at hundreds of universities, colleges and schools of nursing in the United States of America, and a member movement of the International Fellowship of Evangelical Students. For information about local and regional activities, write Public Relations Dept., InterVarsity Christian Fellowship/USA, 6400 Schroeder Rd., P.O. Box 7895, Madison, WI 53707-7895, or visit the IVCF website at <www.ivcf.org>.

Scripture quotations, unless otherwise noted, are from the New Revised Standard Version of the Bible, copyright 1989 by the Division of Christian Education of the National Council of Churches of Christ in the USA.. Used by permission. All rights reserved.

Design: Cindy Kiple
Images: plant with birds: The New York Public Library/ Art Resource, NY
        background: Peter Zelei/ istockphoto

ISBN 978-0-8308-3511-9

Printed in the United States of America ∞

Library of Congress Cataloging-in-Publication Data

Kang, Choonmin.
  Deep-rooted in Christ: the way of transformation / Joshua Choonmin Kang.
      p. cm.
  ISBN-13: 978-0-8308-3511-9 (pbk.: alk. paper)
  1. Spiritual formation—Meditations. 2. Spirituality—Meditations.
  I. Title.
  BV4511.K35 2006
  248.4—dc22

                                                                        2007026750

P 20 19 18 17 16 15 14 13 12 11 10 9 8 7 6 5

Y 23 22 21 20 19 18 17 16 15 · 14 13 12 11 10 09 08

To my praying mother

Contents

Foreword

I encountered Joshua Choonmin Kang the person before I encountered Joshua Choonmin Kang the writer. In fact, our first meeting was not dependent on words at all. I had heard about Pastor Kang and the high regard in which he was held in both Korea and the Korean diaspora. It was almost a reverence at his spiritual depth and quiet authority.

On a Sunday night I was to speak to the congregation he is pastor of, but I went unannounced, alone and without a translator, to the daybreak service beginning at 5:20. My hope was to go beyond the Korean words in order to hear where the words came from.

Please understand, I was not looking to see if the words came from the heart as well as the head, a good thing to be sure. But I was seeking a deeper, more profound source—I was looking to see if this was a person who nurtured the heart before God. Believe me, I was not disappointed. Indeed, I was moved beyond my ability to express.

The church, Oriental Mission Church, is crammed into "Koreatown," one of the neighborhoods in the middle of Los Angeles. More than a thousand folk pack into each of the three Sunday services, stretching the facilities beyond their limit.

That Sunday morning I saw three things, things that in all my travels I almost never find in one person. I saw a man who had soaked himself in prayer and drenched himself in Scripture, and I saw a man who had a genuine pastoral care for his people. By "genuine pastoral care" I mean a pastor who stood before God on behalf of his people, who stood with them in their suffering and who stood committed to their soul growth. These are the things I saw that morning.

Since then my experience of Pastor Kang has been confirmed, even doubled and tripled. What a joy to know a person of such deep character formation, of such quiet authority, of such intense holiness! Whenever I am with him—praying and sharing in the hush of his study, walking and talking with him along the bustling streets of Koreatown or eating and laughing with him at Korean restaurants without number—I feel a compassionate strength and gentle authority flowing from him. Ministering the Word of life, he and I together, in Korean settings throughout the United States (and in Korea itself) is a privilege and an honor.

And now I meet Joshua Choonmin Kang through his writings. *Deep-Rooted in Christ*, the first of his two dozen books to appear in English translation, is a treasure. It reminds me of the gentle spiritual direction of the classic spiritual writers. On the Protestant side, the writings of Andrew Murray, A. W. Tozer and Oswald Chambers. On the Catholic side, François Fénelon and Thomas à Kempis and the letters of Francis of Assisi to Sister Clare. That is to say, Pastor Kang's book is spiritual wisdom literature of the highest order.

Deep-Rooted in Christ speaks to the heart. It urges, gently but ever so persistently, that our hearts should always be turning, turning into the light of Christ, turning toward the Lover of our souls, turning into the Way and the Truth and the Life—"till by turning, turning we come round right." At the same time this book warms the heart, constantly drawing and encouraging, never pushing and condemning.

Deep-Rooted in Christ is, in one sense, a Korean's version of my *Celebration of Discipline*. Or perhaps it is more accurate to say that *Celebration* is an English version of *Deep-Rooted in Christ,* for the Korean original antedates my own writings. Whichever, the themes of both books echo each another. It is moving to witness the common stress on spiritual disciplines that are well recognized worldwide, disciplines of solitude and simplicity and service and meditation and study and prayer and worship and so many more— as the means of God's grace for the transformation of the human personality.

In addition, Pastor Kang's counsels are so sane, so practical. Listen to this simple counsel for those who carry on a lonely vigil in the Sahara of the heart—"A waiting moment will never be a wasted moment." Or consider these wise words of direction to those seeking to lead in the Christian community—"Christian leadership rises from bended knees, tearful eyes and broken hearts."

I began the year 1996 with an extended meditation on John 11, the story of the resurrection of Lazarus. In May of that year I traveled to Korea, still meditating daily on John 11. Many and varied were my experiences in that country; intensive times on prayer mountains and special meetings along the demilitarized zone and myriad morning prayer meetings. Toward the end of my trip a small congregation gave me a parting gift of twenty-four long-stemmed roses.

The next morning, back in Colorado, I sat down to read and to ponder once again John 11, the story of the resurrection of Lazarus. The roses of yesterday lay on the coffee table, already beginning to wilt. Then the *debar Yahweh*, the word of the Lord, came to me indicating that the church is like those roses—some still blooming but others wilting because their stems had been severed from their roots.

At the immense sadness of this reality I began to weep, for I knew it to be so. But then I heard a word of hope, a word of resurrection: "I will raise my church, but first the root system must be reestablished." It was only then that I understood.

All that I had been learning among these good people of Korea about a life of prayer *is* the root system. What we desperately need today is not prayer experiences that we can turn on or off at will like a faucet, but prayer as a constant-flowing life. Then God made it unmistakably clear to me that he has freely chosen to use the peoples of Korea to teach the worldwide Christian family about how to develop the root system of prayer. I speak here of both Korea of the south and Korea of the north. (Though the north has yet to experience God's visitation, it will, in God's time and in God's way.)

The urgent need for us in the West is humility of heart to listen and to learn. And if we are willing to listen and to learn, our Korean brothers and sisters will teach us about a life of prayer that is abundant indeed. *Deep-Rooted in Christ* is just such a teaching. May we listen and learn!

Richard Foster

Preface

I live in two worlds, the East and the West. I communicate in two languages, the one Eastern, the other Western. I also have two streams of spirituality flowing within me, Asian and American. I was born and raised in Korea and have lived in the United States for the last twenty-five years.

As a Korean-American I think in two ways. Sometimes I see a thing as a whole, and sometimes I see only a detail. When I see a tree, yes, I see the whole tree, but sometimes I think only about its roots. When I greet the snow in winter, I see the seed of spring enveloped in it. When I embrace pain, I see, or try to see, the seed of joy that is wrapped inside the pain. When I'm confronted with the problems of life, I tend to look within for the seeds of a solution.

On the one hand, I'm Asian, and my spirituality comes from the East. When I eat fruit, I think about its seed. When I look at the fruit seed, I see a harvest of fruit. When I think of an oak, I see an acorn. When I look at an acorn, I see a forest of oaks. When a pinecone falls, the universe tumbles. When a leaf quivers, the universe trembles. When dew drops, the planets plummet.

On the other hand, I'm American, and my spirituality comes from the West. I've learned the faith and culture of the American people. I've been privileged to meet well-disciplined spiritual leaders and learned much from them about deep spirituality. At the same time, I've learned many creative and practical principles of ministry from the fastest-growing churches.

Yes, I love the abstract, and yet I love the concrete. I've learned not only the know-why (principles) but also the know-how (methodologies). I've acquired the spirituality that fulfills my inner life and the leadership that expands my church life.

While living in two worlds that are often at odds with each other, I've learned how to bring harmony out of conflict. Inevitably, the meeting point, the balancing point, the unifying point is Jesus Christ. Jesus Christ is the language in which the East and the West converse. He is the Lord of all things. He is the Creator of the heavens and earth with his Word. He is the Way, the Truth and the Life.

His love, mercy, kindness, peace, reconciliation and forgiveness are the parts of speech in the common language. In him anyone can love and everyone can communicate.

Yes, Jesus is the language. He is the Word, and yet his language has no words; there is no need for words. If this can indeed be said, then it's the language of silence. Silence is the password that gains entrance to the holy place wherein we worship God in our inner world. And who greets us at the gate? It is Jesus himself.

Deep things are good. Deep taste, deep thought, deep writings, deep words, deep looks, deep love. Often depth is hidden from our sight. However, we feel it, we know it, we reveal it to the rest of the world by the sort of life we lead. As Richard Foster says in his book *Celebration of Discipline*, "The desperate need today is not for a greater number of intelligent people, or gifted people, but deep people."

Needless to say, we don't start our spiritual lives as deep people.

First we have to choose this course of action, and then to grow in the virtue we have to work hard. That doesn't mean we need to be serious all the time. Deep brightness, deep cleanliness, deep refreshment and a bright but deep smile—these are all good things, the sort of things that illumine the spiritual life.

With this book I'd like to invite you into the deeper life that is rooted in Jesus. Pursuing depth takes little enough effort, but it will eventually lead us to a very genuine and very deep inner world.

It is my prayer that as you read this book you will become a person who pursues character before success, integrity before popularity, maturity before growth and service to others before accomplishment in your own life.

Let us go before the Lord Jesus who is the root of humankind. Let us be one in Jesus with his language. Let us accept his lovely invitation. Let us go deeper into the spiritual inner world together.

PART ONE

Beginning

I

Begin with Emptiness

Most of us long for transformation but are afraid to change. Yet spiritual formation begins when we empty our lives. Our spiritual formation begins not with fullness but with emptiness. That's the way we follow Jesus, who "emptied himself, taking the form of a slave, being born in human likeness" (Philippians 2:7).

Even Jesus had to make space for God's action in his life. He had a privileged status, but he relinquished it; he let it go. It's the same with us. We have to empty ourselves. Only then can we begin to be filled up with the blessings of God.

What do we mean by emptying ourselves? How can we connect with this need to give ourselves away?

Let's look first at the figure of Abraham. Abraham began by departing, by leaving home in response to God's command. His departure wasn't just a matter of location. He had to abandon whatever he knew best: his safe haven, his comfort zone.

This is what God is asking us to do as well. He wants us to let go of our old country and enter into the new life he has in mind for us. But abandoning our comfort zones can be terrifying. When we let go of the world we know, we're going to experience pain, suffering and fear.

Many of us who are Korean know what it is like to leave a homeland. We know our own stories and those of others, describing what it is to leave the place we knew best. What a land journey we've made! But our *spiritual* journey isn't only geographic. It's much more than traveling in time and space.

Departing isn't only a matter of location. It's not just leaving one place to go to another. The letting go takes place in the spiritual realm. That is where the deeper journey is made. This deeper journey is a life-passage of abandonment: letting go of our old ways to find the new; emptying ourselves as preparation for receiving the grace God will pour into us.

Abraham can encourage us when we see how he trusted in God.

He was ordered to offer his son Isaac as a sacrifice. Isaac was the promise of God. He was God's promise fulfilled. And so he became Abraham's love, his passion. But it seems that his love for his son took over his heart, taking precedence over his love for God. So God's command to sacrifice the boy was really a call for Abraham to refocus his heart on God.

Abraham had to empty his heart. He had filled his heart with something other than God. And when he did so, he made room, room for God's abundant blessing. He became a friend of God through surrender.

Abraham is the first biblical story about relinquishment, but certainly not the last. He tasted what God the Father would experience when he allowed his Son to die on the cross. The Father's heart was filled with the Son he loved, but he emptied his heart for our sakes to gain the salvation of humankind.

In this same way many great leaders became God's servants. They emptied themselves, abandoned themselves, filled their hearts with nothing but God. And when they departed for the next world, we found the great imprints they left in this world.

Recall the story of Moses. He relinquished his right to be the son of Pharaoh's daughter, and what happened? He became a prophet of God.

Remember the apostles who followed Jesus. "Follow me, and I will make you fish for people" (Matthew 4:19). And what did they do? They abandoned their boats and their fathers' ways. And what did they gain? The kingdom of heaven.

We too must open our hands and let go. For the sake of eternal blessings, we must give up earthly things.

The great missionary Jim Elliot said it well. People who exchange what they can't keep to gain what they can't lose are no fools.

Are our hands clasped too tightly around what we already have? Will we never receive the great things God wants to give us?

To catch the blessings God tosses our way every day, we simply have to open our hands, stretch out our arms.

2

Let Yourself Be Filled

Eastern meditation emphasizes abandonment. Such meditation has total relinquishment as its aim. To the Asian mystics the highest stage of enlightenment is complete self-emptying.

For Christians, however, emptying isn't the end of the story; it's just the beginning. Jesus emptied himself so he could be filled to overflowing. As John said in his Gospel, "The Word became flesh and lived among us, and we have seen his glory, the glory as of a father's only son, full of grace and truth" (John 1:14).

The grace and truth the Father poured into Jesus flowed into other lives as well. As Paul wrote in his letter to the Colossians, "In him all the fullness of God was pleased to dwell" (Colossians 1:19).

What can we learn from this? Notice how Jesus shared his gifts with others. His life was a channel of grace from the Father, a life poured out in service and love. What he received from his Father he gave away. And his disciples did the same. They let the blessings of Jesus flow through their lives to nourish the whole community. And the result was wonderful to behold. More and more became disciples. Communities of Christians grew in size and number. In our own day discipleship grows in the same way.

True ministry begins not with giving but with receiving. We need to be filled up before we have anything to give to others. John told us that "God was pleased to have all his fullness dwell in him" (Colossians 1:19 NIV). We should be pleased to be channels for God's truth and grace.

Many servants of God, acting out of good will, move too quickly into ministry. They focus on giving before they've been refilled and reenergized. They become exhausted before they know it.

There's a lesson here for those who want to give away what they haven't yet received. Let's not be impatient or overeager. Let's wait for our reservoirs to fill with grace.

Have you heard about the dam that was built beside a reservoir? The engineers allowed three years for the reservoir to be filled. During that time they never opened the dam once. Our lives should be like that reservoir. We need patience till it's filled to overflowing.

We should focus on receiving. People who receive are considered great in the kingdom of God. The Bible speaks often of them. There's a certain fullness about them. They are filled to overflowing with abundant grace. Many are found in the Acts of the apostles.

So let's wait for the fullness of Jesus and be completely filled up with him. Then we will be truly satisfied. Diving into the depths of this fullness is what spiritual formation is all about.

That's our ministry, to be filled to the brim, followed by a majestic overflow, sharing Jesus with others.

3

Send the Roots Deep

Balance can be difficult, but it is essential to the deep-rooted life. The best example of the harmony we need is Jesus himself. In him we see perfect balance between emptiness and fullness, between relinquishing and filling. He kept an ideal balance between self-abandonment and exaltation, between serving others and being served by others.

We shouldn't overemphasize either emptiness or fullness. We need a healthy balance between the two. Here's an example. If we leave home too often, we become wanderers. Our lives become unstable. But if we focus on staying put, we get stuck in our ways. Neither extreme is healthy.

The same is true in our spiritual lives. We may enjoy the coolness and sweetness of a meditative pool, but we may stagnate if we stay there too long. Flowing water doesn't stagnate, nor does the active side of spiritual life. It's steady and strong, but may cause erosion. Extremes are what we must watch out for.

Jesus enjoyed his solitude, but he was also at home in a crowd. He was balanced. The time that he spent alone prepared him for the times he spent with people. In the same way, his time in the crowds prepared him for the refreshment of solitude.

Emptying and filling, that was the rhythm of Jesus' life, and so it should be ours. In a very real sense the Christian life is like a pitcher; it's not something in which to store blessings up; it's a vessel out of which to pour blessings from.

This is how it should be with us. But when we don't share with others, our lives decline. Yes, filling has just one purpose: sharing. Jesus' life was filled to overflowing so that it could be shared with others.

Jesus' life wasn't like the Dead Sea, a stagnant lake where even fish can't survive. His life was like the Sea of Galilee that empties into the Jordan, teeming with life.

The heart of Jesus is like that Sea of Galilee. Our lives can be the same: filled with satisfaction and joy. The joy comes when we share as Jesus did. Joy flows in us when we pour out what God has given us.

Isaiah's prophecies showed the Messiah as both a flowing stream and a great rock (Isaiah 32:2). How can one person be both rock and stream? These poetic comparisons in Scripture suggest the harmony and balance in the way Jesus lived.

The life of Jesus was like flowing water, descending from higher ground. This flowing water heads downstream, fulfilling its destiny, finding its way, till it empties at last into the ocean.

That way of flowing was the Jesus way of living, not fighting or competing but submitting to what his Father asked of him. Yes, his life ended on the cross—to gain the world's salvation. But look at the whole story.

Jesus is also like a rock: unshakable. He didn't waver. When Satan tempted him, he didn't give in. In every challenge he went ahead to the destiny the Father had prepared for him.

On the one hand, he's living water. On the other hand, he's solid rock. To be both rock and water is to live in harmony and balance, as Jesus did.

Let's look at Jesus as both the lion and the lamb. In Revelation 5, John describes Jesus in perfect balance between two seemingly opposite extremes. He came as the suffering lamb, spotless and blameless in every way. But he is also the royal lion who rules the whole universe. Willingly submitting to nature's laws, he also had the power to overcome these laws.

Jesus offers to us the same sort of balance and harmony. When we're willing to engage in the disciplines of the spiritual life, this balance can be ours. Balance is all-important when it comes to serving God. It's what God wants for us.

We must try to be like Jesus. He shows us how to submit and how to rule. Like him, we should maintain a perfectly balanced walk. We walk with him. We run with him. We imitate him in every way. This may leave us at the end of our race out of breath but with no regrets.

PART TWO

Becoming Rooted in Jesus

4

Can Bad Roots
Bring Good Fruit?

Human beings live in two worlds at once, the conscious world and the unconscious world. Below the surface, in the unconscious world, some of the most severe problems lie. It's what lies below the proverbial "tip of the iceberg." If there's melting on the top, then that's the sure sign that there's melting below the surface of the water.

Spiritual disciplines can help us with the deep, inner life of the soul. The inner life is where God lives and where we have conversation with God. There we meet God in sweet fellowship. But sometimes, if the root is sick, the whole tree (that is to say, our whole life) has a problem. By maintaining healthy spiritual disciplines, we identify the source of our problems. Then we cooperate with God who solves them through the power of the Holy Spirit.

When a plant is unhealthy, we look for reasons. Is it getting too much water? Not enough water? Does it need more sun or more shade? Are insects eating away at the plant? Sometimes the problem is obvious, sometimes it isn't.

Andrew Murray, Scottish missionary and devotional writer in

the nineteenth century, warned in *The Inner Life* that a spiritual
life, though it appeared healthy on the surface, may have con-
tracted a "root disease." South African orange trees were particularly susceptible to such a phenomenon. They looked healthy and
still produced what looked like healthy fruit. The casual observer
doesn't notice any trouble, but an expert can recognize the beginning of slow death.

From this botanical disease, *phylloxera*, named after the destruc-
tive insect, Murray makes a spiritual comparison. There's no radical
cure, he says, but to take out the old roots and provide new ones. A
graft from a healthy root can help. In due time it will produce the
same stem and branches as before, but now with a new resistance
to disease. Murray is speaking of the "part of the plant that is hidden from sight . . . where healing must be sought."

As with plants, so with us. Life's problems begin in the root system of the soul. By the time we notice them, our souls may be very
sick indeed. The pain of the soul is worse than any we suffer from
bodily injuries. But there's hope. We can restore and maintain the
health of our souls by being constantly on watch.

A pastor's wife in Chicago nearly died of leukemia. I remember
the situation well; we prayed together. After receiving many hospi-
tal treatments, she was told by the doctors that her life was quite
fragile, her immune system was very weak. But she overcame this
overwhelming problem. Later she even gave birth to a beautiful
baby girl named Sarah.

According to God's word in Proverbs, "The human spirit will
endure sickness, but a broken spirit—who can bear?" (Proverbs
18:14). Also Proverbs teaches us that "a cheerful heart is a good
medicine, but a downcast spirit dries up the bones" (Proverbs
17:22).

Often we exercise to overcome our physical weaknesses; seldom do we pay the same attention to our souls. Bodily health doesn't solve spiritual problems. Even if we recover from one disease, we may contract another.

All humans are destined to die. A healthy soul, however, strengthens us both in this life and in eternity.

The moral? Life's problems are best solved at the root level; that's where we care for our souls; that's where the medicine is spiritual discipline.

5

Becoming Rooted in Jesus

✿

It's one thing to experience the spiritual world. It's quite another thing to live the disciplined life. Sometimes it's hard to separate the two, but there is a clear, identifiable difference.

Spiritual experiences are like fires burning in a forest. We can almost see them, hear them, smell them. They feel like power coming down from above. We know they bring blessings.

Spiritual experiences attract us. They draw our interest. Often, we're blessed with them before we even know what they are. This may be a personal or a community experience, but one we certainly don't expect. Yet simply by being in certain places and joining certain communities, we know the power of God's ministry in our lives.

Yes, the kingdom of God comes in power. Only through God's power is Satan thwarted. Only through God's power is God's Word implanted in human hearts.

If these experiences are true, how do they differ from spiritual disciplines?

Spiritual experiences and spiritual disciplines are similar, but they have different outcomes. It's good to desire wonderful spiritual experiences, but it's better to desire a deep inner life with God.

God wants his life to penetrate the depths of your being. When this happens, your transformation is occurring through glorious revelation. But this doesn't happen overnight. Instead you may expect to spend long, arduous periods of practicing spiritual disciplines as you are developing an inward Christlike character.

Spiritual formation isn't like a quickly spreading fire; it's like a tree with deeply descending roots, establishing a foundation for future growth and fruitfulness. Through the disciplines each one of us becomes a fruitful tree, a place for birds to nest, a resting place for others. So God uses our lives to bear quiet but abundant fruit.

Too many modern churches want powerful experiences from above; sadly, they show little interest in becoming deeply rooted in God. The church in Korea is one such example. After it was founded, it spread all over Korea like wildfire. Obviously, it was due to the great and powerful work of the Spirit. But for many this newfound faith was lacking a firm foundation, and a spiritual void followed. The new Christians were looking for temporal spiritual power; they should have been concentrating on being more like Jesus.

Because of this spiritual void many Korean churches experimented with Bible-study programs and discipleship plans. Sadly, these programs were little more than church-growth strategies. That's when these churches began to reconsider the significance of spiritual formation.

In Colossians the apostle Paul had this to say about the path to a deeper spiritual life. "As you . . . have received Christ Jesus the Lord, continue to live your lives in him, rooted and built up in him and established in the faith, just as you were taught, abounding in thanksgiving" (Colossians 2:6-7).

When we have strong, deep roots in Christ, we'll have peace and comfort that can withstand the storms of life. When we develop spiritual disciplines, we dive into another dimension. We must develop root systems for the inner life; they will connect us to Jesus Christ. He's the source of all power and the one who gives life.

6

Christic Is the Firm Foundation

Let's explore another comparison that Jesus used.

As we develop spiritual disciplines, we resemble the wise builder who sets out to make a tall building to please God. The first and perhaps most important thing is to construct a foundation strong enough to support the tall building. Shoddy work will bring down the tallest building, no matter how beautiful it may be. Foundations must be deep and strong, able to withstand the stress of height and weight. Giant skyscrapers may adorn the world's great cities but only when their foundations are able to stand the stress.

How can we build a life that won't collapse under stress? We build it on the firm foundation of Jesus Christ.

In his first letter to the Corinthians, Paul emphasized the need for a firm foundation:

> According to the grace of God given to me, like a skilled master builder I laid a foundation, and someone else is building on it. Each builder must choose with care how to build on it. For no one can lay any foundation other than the one that has been laid; that foundation is Jesus Christ. (1 Corinthians 3:10-11)

For the ancient Israelites as well as for modern builders, the cornerstone has been critically important. It was first of the foundation stones laid and truly gave support to the structure. Without such a stone a building would crumble.

Jesus is our foundation in the Christian life. Too often people build their lives on the shaky foundations of philosophy, self-reliance, human morality, ethics, wealth, power, self-interest and self-empowerment. Things like these may seem important from a worldly viewpoint. But if we see life from an eternal perspective, our whole outlook changes. From the eternal vantage point, such foundations are as short-lived as the grass of the field.

Seeking spiritual formation is like taking hold of the eternal foundation, seeing everything in the light of eternity. When we do that, we focus on what lasts instead of what passes away; not on worldly things but on God's kingdom. That's when the kingdom of God rules our inner world.

Seeking a deeper spiritual life means laying a deep foundation in Christ. In a strong gale a building may sway, but because of its strong foundation it holds fast. A well-crafted ship holds steady even in heavy seas. The same is true in the spiritual realm.

A truly spiritual life isn't built on things that are seen but on things that are unseen.

In recent years we have witnessed two terrible disasters in Korea. In the city of Seoul, both the Sam Poong department store and the Song Soo bridge collapsed. Hundreds were killed. They were handsome structures, but apparently their foundations had hidden faults. Apparently the builders had used cheap materials and wanted quick results. Beauty couldn't save the buildings; they came tumbling down.

Johann Wolfgang von Goethe, the renowned nineteenth-century German poet, is quoted as saying, "If you start your buttons from the wrong hole, you won't have a hole for the last button." Does this seem like a light remark from such a serious writer? Yes, but his witticism contains a vitally important truth.

Where we begin is vital. It's better to build correctly than to build quickly. The wider road may not be the better road. Even broad superhighways have their limitations; commuters still wind up in traffic jams.

To choose the path of spiritual discipline, however, is to choose the narrow path. So let us keep first things first. We must invest time and energy to build a solid foundation for living. This careful approach will lead to sounder discipleship in Christ.

7

Minding the Inner Life

Real energy comes from a strong inner life. Remember the Samaritan woman? Jesus said to her, "Those who drink of the water that I will give them will never be thirsty. The water that I will give will become in them a spring of water gushing up to eternal life" (John 4:14).

Jesus is the One who gives us a spring of water welling up to eternal life. The Lord wants to bestow grace on us, but he also wants us to experience this blessedness.

Jesus condemned the Pharisees as white-washed tombs; they seemed godly on the outside, but they lacked authentic righteousness on the inside. We too may walk around with a big Bible in each hand, but that doesn't prove we are godly. Pay attention to what is really welling up in your inner world.

Paul had this to say to the Ephesians. "I pray that, according to the riches of his glory, he may grant that you may be strengthened in your inner being" (Ephesians 3:16). Paul's intercessory prayer should be ours as well.

The powerful presence of the Holy Spirit should bring dramatic changes to our inner world. Spiritual formation isn't a matter of outward change; it originates with change in our inner world. To grasp this we must understand the essence of learning.

The word *educate* has a root meaning: "to lead out from within." Spiritual education isn't about packing knowledge or information into our hearts. It's about letting God transform us from the inside out. What a precious treasure we Christians have received! The Holy Spirit dwells in us so that our inner worlds may be transformed.

Let us not forget what God told Samuel: "Do not look on his appearance or on the height of his stature, because I have rejected him; for the LORD does not see as mortals see; they look on the outward appearance, but the LORD looks on the heart" (1 Samuel 16:7).

A beautiful outward appearance may be an asset. What really matters, however, is our inner world. That determines who we really are. God looks beyond our human appearances; he sees through the disguises we put on. The Lord searches deep within our hearts and sees us as we really are.

Paul's letters deal extensively with the inner world. His words to the Galatians continue to ring sorrowfully in my heart. "My little children, for whom I am again in the pain of childbirth until Christ is formed in you" (Galatians 4:19).

Do you notice Paul's emphasis on the way God works in our lives? He says that Christ must be "formed in you." The Lord wants to work in our inner world. He is not out to adjust our outward appearance. Jesus transforms the inner character. When we focus on outward appearances we can't experience genuine transformation.

In short, spiritual formation is about cultivating the inner world, which is hidden from the people we know. Spiritual formation means cultivating the heart. In his first letter Peter reminds us to notice the inward character of our lives: "Rather, let your adornment be the inner self with the lasting beauty of a gentle and quiet spirit, which is very precious in God's sight" (1 Peter 3:4).

What a division we find in our inner selves! Jeremiah put it into words.

> The heart is devious above all else;
>   it is perverse—
> who can understand it? (Jeremiah 17:9)

Such is the human condition. But Proverbs shows us there is also a hopeful side of the human heart:

> Keep your heart with all vigilance,
> for from it flow the springs of life. (Proverbs 4:23)

So two opposing impulses reside in our hearts: both sinister darkness and heavenly light. Earthly things dwell there, things that contradict God, and also spiritual things that bring forth peace. To cultivate this inner being, we must take time to make keen observations. Spiritual discipline involves the careful cultivation of the heart. Without it we cannot present pure hearts to God.

8

Spiritual Discipline
and the Deep Well

Living water forms a deep well in every believer's heart. In other words, the work of God is being accomplished deep in the Christian's heart. The Holy Spirit himself is the source of this deep well. He's the living water deep in our hearts.

The purest fountains come from the deepest wells. A fountain from a shallow well brings forth diluted water, water mixed with dirt. A shallow well fills up during a rainy season, but a dry season will dry it right up. A deep well is untouched by changes of climate. Even in the scorching heat of summer, deep well water is cool. In the freezing cold winter the well water stays pure. No matter how conditions change, the deep well yields water that is crystal clear.

Christians empowered by the Holy Spirit are fed from a very deep well. They don't fluctuate or change. When we are filled with the Holy Spirit, our inner world is stable in spite of the shifting world outside. Christians are deepened by the trials they undergo. They rise above their challenges. Environment doesn't dictate their behavior; instead, they transform the environment they live in.

Christians who practice spiritual disciplines have a divine conspiracy in their hearts. As Paul tells the Colossians, God has given them abundant wisdom and knowledge (Colossians 2:3). Proverbs tells us that "the purposes in the human mind are like deep water, / but the intelligent will draw them out" (Proverbs 20:5).

The Word of God clarifies our vision and reminds us that God blesses us generously with his precious knowledge. Those who believe in Jesus have everything in the world. Jesus lives in them; his knowledge abides in them. Our challenge is to draw out that divine power.

The wise person knows how to draw on the deep in the well of his or her inner life. If we're wise, we know that worldly wealth isn't true wealth; external success should never be our aim. Instead, we should look for spiritual treasure: treasure that comes from a godly character that the Holy Spirit develops within us.

The beauty of a wise person shows through the words he or she decides to speak. Proverbs says, "the words of the mouth are deep waters; / the fountain of wisdom is a gushing stream" (Proverbs 18:4).

Deep thoughts spring up from the hidden places of the heart. Words from the inner depth of our hearts don't get lost in space; instead, they make an impact on the lives of others. In this way our inner worlds become intertwined.

Spiritual depth shows itself in this remarkable way. Sometimes when we speak from the heart, others feel they are hearing their own inner thoughts expressed. So words can connect us to one another, both outwardly and inwardly. They can revive our souls. Words this deep come only from the practice of deep spiritual disciplines.

PART THREE

Growing in Grace

9

Plumbing the Depths

There is a hidden world: a world we cannot see. That's where God is calling us to come. He's calling us to take part in deeper things, spiritual things. He wants us to set out for deep waters. As David writes in one of his psalms:

> Deep calls to deep
> at the thunder of your cataracts;
> all your waves and your billows
> have gone over me. (Psalm 42:7)

Jesus instructed Peter to "put out into the deep water and let down your nets for a catch" (Luke 5:4).

The purpose of a ship isn't to stay docked in the harbor. Our human souls weren't made for shallow water. We must dive into deeper waters with the help of the Holy Spirit. In these deep places the wonderful treasures of the spiritual life are found.

Of course it is easier to stay in our own comfort zones. But when we abandon ourselves by faith to the unknown spiritual depths we make a first step toward being transformed by love. There in those deep places we'll be challenged, changed, transformed.

True Christian maturity is defined in terms of the inner world.

How can we truly know a person if we only see his or her outer world? Possessions, behaviors, actions, words? All these are superficial. Only in the inward places of the heart will we know each other and ourselves. Christ is leading us there.

Richard J. Foster, devotional writer and founder of the spiritual movement Renovaré, put his finger on it when he said in *Celebration of Discipline:* "The desperate need today is not for a greater number of intelligent people, or gifted people, but deep people."

What does he mean by the term *deep people?* The answer is rather simple. Deep people are those who practice spiritual disciplines in depth. Deep people have close relationships with God, who is Spirit.

This is the nature of the inner world. The Holy Spirit ministers there. The Word penetrates us there.

Proverbs tells us "the human spirit is the lamp of the LORD, / searching every inmost part" (Proverbs 20:27). Meditate on these words. What do they imply? That there are places in our inner world where God must come to cultivate our souls.

Spiritual maturity comes when our spiritual lives are cultivated. How does this happen? How do we enter the deep places of the spiritual world? What brings us into depth and maturity?

First of all, it is the Word. The Word of God is the only tool that can bring about our spiritual formation. The author of Hebrews tells us: "Indeed, the word of God is living and active, sharper than any two-edged sword, piercing until it divides soul from spirit, joints from marrow; it is able to judge the thoughts and intentions of the heart" (Hebrews 4:12). Only the Word of God can pierce the soul and spirit. Only the Word of God can judge the thoughts and desires of the heart.

Second, the Holy Spirit is what brings us to maturity and depth.

The Holy Spirit can do a deep work in Christian hearts. Paul said, "These things God has revealed to us through the Spirit; for the Spirit searches everything, even the depths of God" (1 Corinthians 2:10).

The Holy Spirit offers us the utmost intimate knowledge of God and of our inward thoughts. He knows the content and condition of our hearts. Unless we abide in the Word and under the power of the Holy Spirit, we can't know the depths that God intends for us.

We must become like deep wells. We must become like living fountains.

10

Growing Through Grace

All spiritual growth is initiated by God. He's the one who causes any transformation a Christian may experience. We depend on his gracious touch. It's the foundation for spiritual life and growth. However, we ourselves must set the stage for the Holy Spirit to work in our lives.

Before a seed is planted, we must first prepare the soil. Later that seed will grow and bear fruit. We are tools in God's hands. But God can use such tools—ourselves—to cultivate his world, to bring transformation in the lives of people everywhere.

Paul clearly understood his role as an instrument of God. He wrote to the church in Corinth where divisions existed among believers, "I planted, Apollos watered, but God gave the growth. So neither the one who plants nor the one who waters is anything, but only God who gives the growth" (1 Corinthians 3:6-7).

Paul isn't downgrading the importance of spiritual leaders, nor questioning the way they help their followers. If Paul hadn't planted and Apollos hadn't watered, how could a church in Corinth have sprouted to life?

What Paul wants to convey in these verses is that transformation only comes through the power of God. He himself experienced that transformation as he was writing those words.

What captivated Paul was the grace of God. He saw that the law couldn't bring about real transformation. Though he himself was "without blemish" according to the law, even so he found himself doing things he didn't want to do; he recognized his own wickedness (Romans 7:15-21).

Paul had no other alternative but to surrender to grace; his will wasn't sufficient to overcome his tendencies. That's how he came to see that only God can bring about authentic transformation. Possibly that's why he was so fond of greeting his readers with the words, "Grace to you and peace from God" (Ephesians 1:2; Philippians 1:2; Colossians 1:2). He writes to the Corinthians in his first letter: "But by the grace of God I am what I am, and his grace toward me has not been in vain. On the contrary, I worked harder than any of them—though it was not I, but the grace of God that is with me" (1 Corinthians 15:10).

Peter had a similar experience with regard to God's grace. He was quick to make promises to Jesus but slow to keep them. He swore by his own life that he wouldn't abandon his Lord, and yet he denied Jesus three times. His sluggish human nature and Satan's influence led him to fail (Matthew 26:41; Luke 22:31-32).

Peter had the brief but terrible experience of being Satan's instrument: a traitor, a renegade and a liar. What could possibly transform a man like that? Only the grace of God. After Peter had failed completely, Jesus forgave his sins. He extended grace and mercy to this helpless, hopeless man and gave him another chance to serve, and by the grace of God Peter became a powerful leader of the apostolic church.

So Peter writes in one of his letters: "Grow in the grace and knowledge of our Lord and Savior Jesus Christ. To him be the glory both now and to the day of eternity. Amen" (2 Peter 3:18).

Notice his emphasis on both knowledge and grace for spiritual growth. Note also that apart from the grace of God spiritual growth is simply impossible.

11

Put Away Childish Things

When someone wants to practice spiritual disciplines, what does that mean? It means the person wants to mature in spirit.

Stages of spiritual maturation are clearly described in the Bible: infancy, youth and adulthood. John referred to all three in his epistles:

> I write to you, children,
>   because you know the Father.
> I write to you, fathers,
>   because you know him who is from the beginning.
> I write to you, young people,
>   because you are strong
>   and the word of God abides in you,
>   and you have overcome the evil one. (1 John 2:14)

Paul urged the Corinthians to abandon their childish behaviors. "When I was a child, I spoke like a child, I reasoned like a child; when I became an adult, I put an end to childish ways" (1 Corinthians 13:11).

He had more to say about this in his letter to the Ephesians: "We must no longer be children, tossed to and fro and blown about by every wind of doctrine, by people's trickery, by their craftiness in deceitful scheming" (Ephesians 4:14).

One common trait of small children is their inability to deal with temptation. They give way to it because they can't tell the difference between good and evil. The ability to distinguish good from evil is a form of wisdom. Our capacity to recognize and avoid evil determines our character.

In the spiritual realm this gift of wise discernment helps us to take hold of spiritual truth. Paul writes in 1 Corinthians: "Brothers and sisters, do not be children in your thinking; rather, be infants in evil, but in thinking be adults" (1 Corinthians 14:20). When Paul used the word *adult* he stressed the importance of having a fully mature capacity to distinguish good from evil.

Where can we find such wisdom? It can be found only in Jesus, "in whom are hidden all the treasures of wisdom and knowledge" (Colossians 2:3). Those who are in Jesus possess spiritual knowledge. To grow into maturity, we must apply this knowledge wisely.

We can find such wisdom by meditating on the Word of God. Such wisdom comes when we meditate on Jesus, his life and his Word. "I have more understanding than all my teachers, / for your decrees are my meditation" (Psalm 119:99).

How can a student outgrow his teacher in knowledge? Only through meditation. The understanding and insight to distinguish good from evil come through meditating on the Word.

Another characteristic of infants is their lack of balance. They totter from one place to another. They walk along peacefully until suddenly—they crash and fall.

Their uncertainty, lack of confidence, is something like the double-mindedness that James noticed among immature believers. He spoke of these spiritual infants this way. "Ask in faith, never doubting, for the one who doubts is like a wave of the sea, driven and tossed by the wind; for the doubter, being double-minded and unstable in every way, must not expect to receive anything from the Lord" (James 1:6-8).

What is meant by spiritual maturity? It's being solidly grounded in one's inner being. Isaiah put it this way. "Those of steadfast mind you keep in peace—in peace because they trust in you" (Isaiah 26:3).

Spiritual living comes from trust in the Lord. When our eyes are fixed on the Lord Jesus and we trust in his Word, we will be steadfast and mature.

12

Growth That Matches Knowledge

Wisdom and spiritual growth are interrelated.

Wisdom has two dimensions: horizontal or worldly wisdom, and vertical or spiritual wisdom.

Worldly wisdom is temporal and changes easily. By contrast, spiritual wisdom stays with us always. It has no limits.

Worldly wisdom teaches us how to live during our stay on earth. It involves such things as common knowledge and etiquette. While those things may have some value in this life, they can't bring about a genuine transformation in us.

Knowledge is wonderful, but accumulating knowledge doesn't guarantee increasing transformation. These days we are overwhelmed by the sheer amount of factual information and knowledge available at any given moment. But that kind of knowledge doesn't make us better people. At best, it produces better informed sinners. They may look impressive, but their inner world is unclean.

On the other hand, vertical wisdom, that is, wisdom that comes from God's Word, trains our lives for blessings, both now and in the world to come. Godly wisdom goes far beyond common sense, beyond practical morality. It makes us more like Jesus Christ, helping us to live not just naturally but supernaturally—as spiritual beings.

God wants us to have spiritual knowledge; the prophet Hosea has told us this (Hosea 6:6). When the ancient Jews raised their children, they trained them to keep a "basket" in their inner world where spiritual wisdom could be stored. Wise as serpents and innocent as doves, Jewish parents reared their children in godliness, using established means of education. God's people have always borne this responsibility: to train their children in spiritual wisdom and knowledge.

Hosea exclaimed,

My people are destroyed for lack of knowledge;
  because you have rejected knowledge,
  I reject you from being a priest to me.
And since you have forgotten the law of your God,
  I also will forget your children. (Hosea 4:6)

Hosea was referring to personal knowledge of God. People who lack this intimate knowledge are doomed to failure. The degree to which we grow in knowledge of God is the degree to which we grow in spiritual maturity. Knowledge of God is our key to a bright future. Without that knowledge we will fail.

Paul explained this truth to the Ephesians: "All of us [will] come to the unity of the faith and of the knowledge of the Son of God, to maturity, to the measure of the full stature of Christ" (Ephesians 4:13).

Peter had similar experiences and valued this principle too, as he said in his second letter: "Grow in the grace and knowledge of our Lord and Savior Jesus Christ. To him be the glory both now and to the day of eternity. Amen" (2 Peter 3:18).

John also expressed the same truth.

If we want to live disciplined spiritual lives, we must diligently search for knowledge of God. The words of Hosea express this:

> Let us know, let us press on to know the LORD;
>> his appearing is as sure as the dawn;
> he will come to us like the showers,
>> like the spring rains that water the earth. (Hosea 6:3)

Storing up knowledge of God is directly linked to receiving God's grace. We can experience God only to the degree to which he makes himself known to us. He reveals himself through his Word and by his Holy Spirit. We'll experience and know God when we read the Word under the guidance of the Holy Spirit. This knowledge of God, or so the psalmist tells us, is so sweet that the Bible invites us to taste it (Psalm 34:8).

13

Grow Through
In-Depth Understanding

In God's economy, lack of understanding causes many problems. In the psalms we read,

> They will go to the company of their ancestors,
>   who will never again see the light. (Psalm 49:19)

What distinguishes us humans from animals? Our innate ability to understand through reason. People who don't have a reasoned understanding are unable to help others. We must first know the truth before we can explain it to someone else. Isaiah's words are helpful here:

> The Lord God has given me
>   the tongue of a teacher,
> that I may know how to sustain
>   the weary with a word.
> Morning by morning he wakens—
>   wakens my ear
>   to listen as those who are taught. (Isaiah 50:4)

Jesus came to reveal the truth. He emphasized understanding

when he taught about the kingdom of God. "The reason I speak to them in parables is that 'seeing they do not perceive, and hearing they do not listen, nor do they understand' " (Matthew 13:13).

Jesus showed us a clear correlation between knowing God's truth and entering God's kingdom. Jesus used the parable of the sower to teach us that Satan will come and attempt to take away the Word once planted in our hearts if we do not understand the truth (Matthew 13:19).

Listen to what Jesus says about the kind of soil that produces good fruit. "As for what was sown on good soil, this is the one who hears the word and understands it, who indeed bears fruit and yields, in one case a hundredfold, in another sixty, and in another thirty" (Matthew 13:23).

One key to bearing good fruit is the ability to hear and understand. Before we can obey God's Word, we have to understand it. When we become obedient to that Word, we may be said to bear good fruit.

What is the source of the good fruit of understanding? It all begins with a seed. God's Word is that seed. The Bible teaches that the Word is the key to understanding spiritual mysteries.

Often understanding comes about through the guidance of a spiritually minded mentor or teacher. When the Ethiopian eunuch met Philip, he was in a chariot, reading about the Word from the book of Isaiah. "Philip ran up to [the chariot] and heard him reading the prophet Isaiah." That is when Philip asked an important question. "Do you understand what you are reading?" (Acts 8:30). Pay close attention to the eunuch's response. "How can I," he said, "unless someone guides me?" (v. 31).

When we meet excellent spiritual guides like Philip, they'll teach us the Word. God has sent gifted teachers to his church.

They have a special role: to identify the way, to know the way and to teach about the way.

Besides all this, the Holy Spirit helps us directly. "The Advocate, the Holy Spirit, whom the Father will send in my name, will teach you everything, and remind you of all that I have said to you" (John 14:26). The Holy Spirit gives light to the Word. The Holy Spirit illuminates those truths that may otherwise be hard to understand. John points out the importance of the Holy Spirit's role: "his anointing teaches you about all things" (1 John 2:27). The Spirit resides within all believers and opens our mind to the deep dimensions of God's Word.

Another essential link to understanding God's Word is prayer. People who pray simply understand the Word better. Daniel gained insight about the seventy years of Babylonian captivity while he was reading the book of Jeremiah (Daniel 9:2). He decided to fast and pray to gain still deeper understanding of the matter (v. 3). God heard his prayer and answered him through his angel. "Do not fear, Daniel, for from the first day that you set your mind to gain understanding and to humble yourself before your God, your words have been heard, and I have come because of your words" (Daniel 10:12). Here Daniel shows himself as a servant of God who wanted understanding. His prayer poured forth from the deep well of his humility. We too should search for understanding through humble prayer.

14

Sharpening
Our Spiritual Vision

One distinguishing mark of maturity is keen perception. The letter to the Hebrews put it this way: "Solid food is for the mature, for those whose faculties have been trained by practice to distinguish good from evil" (Hebrews 5:14). A grown adult can discern the truth. God trains his children in discernment through hard trials that help us mature. That's how mature believers come to know the difference between good and evil.

A mature servant of God should have this power of discernment. The word *faith* has become trivial to many because it has been used so carelessly. The Bible doesn't call us to some form of blind faith. Blind faith is not the real faith that God wants from us. He calls us to biblical faith, which has a clear object and content. True, godly faith involves a way of seeing that comes only through knowledge.

Mature Christian faith involves the marriage of belief and wisdom. Paul gives an admonition along these lines to his beloved son in Christ, Timothy: "Do your best to present yourself to God as one approved by him, a worker who has no need to be ashamed, rightly explaining the word of truth" (2 Timothy 2:15). To understand the Word effectively, we must be sharp and perceptive. We must become skilled thinkers.

Many of our problems come from sloth. In *The Road Less Traveled*, Scott Peck defines original sin as "sloth in thinking abilities." When Satan approached Adam and Eve and planted doubts about the Word of God, they reacted without having second thoughts. They wouldn't have submitted to Satan's temptation if they had carefully considered his words. If they had tested and analyzed Satan's words, the outcome would have been completely different.

Yes, the foundation of original sin can be traced back to sloth in thinking. Paul put it this way in his second letter to the Corinthians. "We destroy arguments and every proud obstacle raised up against the knowledge of God, and we take every thought captive to obey Christ" (2 Corinthians 10:4-5). Before we can make all our thoughts obedient to Jesus, we must first know how to analyze them and gain deeper knowledge about them.

Judas's great betrayal can also be linked to lazy thinking. John writes of Judas Iscariot at the Last Supper. "The devil had already put it into the heart of Judas son of Simon Iscariot to betray him" (John 13:2). Judas was overwhelmed by the idea of turning Jesus over to Satan; he couldn't allow his mind to obey Jesus. It all came down to this: he didn't discipline his mind.

Competitive athletes must train their physical bodies; serious Christian thinkers must rigorously train their minds. To discipline our physical bodies, we train until it hurts. Take a well-disciplined swimmer. He or she can experience success and enjoy freedom in the water. Once we undergo hard training, liberty greets us on the other end. Ultimately, our level of conditioning will depend on our well-disciplined training regimen.

Great thoughts work the same way. They rarely come overnight; they are the result of disciplined thinking. Our capacity for great thinking is increased through study, synthesis and reflection on the information we have gathered. If we go through such a process, we can avoid many great problems.

Gordon McDonald has this to say in *Ordering Your Private World:* "Thinking is a great work. It is best done with a mind that has trained and is in shape." For disciplined training of our thoughts, constant study and reading are our greatest tools.

As we train our minds to think, we should never forget our real purpose. Our ultimate objective in training our minds is to give glory and honor to God. That is the goal of all spiritual discipline.

15

Growing from
a Lamb to a Lion

Scripture depicts Jesus metaphorically as both a lion and a lamb. When we look at his life, we easily see the characteristics of each one. He died like a gentle lamb on the cross; at the same time he reigned above all as a kingly lion (Revelation 5:6).

Isaiah described the lamb this way:

> He was oppressed, and he was afflicted,
>   yet he did not open his mouth;
> like a lamb that is led to the slaughter,
>   and like a sheep that before its shearers is silent,
>   so he did not open his mouth. (Isaiah 53:7)

However, Jesus was the king. When Pontius Pilate asked Jesus, "Are you the king of the Jews?" Jesus answered, "You say so" (Matthew 27:11). At the command of Jesus even the roaring sea obeyed; death let go its grip at the sound of his words. Mountains and streams bowed before him. Jesus ruled heaven and earth and is the king of all kings (Matthew 28:18).

To some there seems to be a contradiction between the characteristics of a lion and a lamb. Yet Jesus lived in complete harmony as both. And though we may be different from Jesus, God wants to see these same contrasting characteristics in us. God calls us lambs:

> All we like sheep have gone astray;
>> we have all turned to our own way,
> and the Lord has laid on him
>> the iniquity of us all. (Isaiah 53:6)

We are like lambs, just as Isaiah describes us. Lambs cannot survive alone; they need shepherds. Lambs are weak and need guidance. When they get lost, they can't find their way home on their own. We humans are the same way, getting lost, needing guidance. We can't exist on our own, apart from God.

Jesus said, "I am the vine, you are the branches. Those who abide in me and I in them bear much fruit, because apart from me you can do nothing" (John 15:5). This is the truth; we can do nothing apart from him. We depend on him for everything. Jesus is the source and sustainer of our very existence. He is like a life rope. Everything comes from the Lord. So all of us are like lambs, but what does it mean to become like a lion?

The lion is king of the jungle; he rules in the animal kingdom. The Bible also describes Christians as destined to rule. We are "a royal priesthood," writes Peter (1 Peter 2:9). "If we endure, we will also reign with him," writes Timothy (2 Timothy 2:12). These words remind us that royal blood is flowing in our veins.

Before God, we need to be like lambs. In our relationship to other believers, we must act with sacrificial love. But against sin, the world and Satan, we have to be like valiant lions.

God gave Jesus power to rule heaven and earth. In our lives we also share in this divine authority (John 1:12). Our Lord gave this authority over to his disciples and us. Luke writes, "Jesus called the twelve together and gave them power and authority over all demons and to cure diseases" (Luke 9:1).

With this same authority we need to learn how to rule in this world. Not only must we adapt to our environment but we also must reign in it; only then will we overcome the influence of Satan in this world. We can't be slaves to sin; we must reign over it. To this effect Paul writes to the Romans, "Much more surely will those who receive the abundance of grace and the free gift of righteousness exercise dominion in life through the one man, Jesus Christ" (Romans 5:17).

Before God, then, we should become gentle lambs, but against this world we must be royal priests, as kingly as lions.

16

Training to Grow in Grace

※

Only by the grace of God can we be transformed and changed. As Richard Foster has said in *Celebration of Discipline,* "The needed change within us is God's work, not ours. The demand is for an inside job, and only God can work from the inside."

A genuine transformation doesn't happen overnight. Fundamental transformation takes place bit by bit; it happens by degrees in our inner world. When this inner transformation is noticed by others, they tend to conclude that the conversion is a real one.

Who brings about this inner formation? Paul answers this question clearly in his letter to the Philippians: "I am confident of this, that the one who began a good work among you will bring it to completion by the day of Jesus Christ" (Philippians 1:6). That is to say, God is the one who began the work in our inner world. But how?

God has implanted hope for the future in our hearts, hope that will lead to our transformation. Paul writes, again to the Philippians: "It is God who is at work in you, enabling you to will and to work for his good pleasure" (Philippians 2:13). David also agrees, "Take delight in the LORD, / and he will give you the desires of your heart" (Psalm 37:4).

God knows where we need to be transformed and plants desire in our hearts to bring that about. What a wonderful and blessed grace this is! For our part, we need to pray that our good hopes and desires may be brought to completion. Putting our faith into practice in our daily lives takes real spiritual discipline.

Spiritual discipline is all about practicing the will that God has put into our hearts. Arid laws come into our mind when we mention practicing our faith. But when we read the Bible carefully, we learn that there are no better spiritual tools than trials and disciplines.

How much of my growth is my own responsibility, and how much of it is the work of God? This confusion was eventually wiped away when I read Colossians: "To this end I labor, struggling with all his energy, which so powerfully works in me" (Colossians 1:29 NIV). This cannot take place with my strength and effort. It can only happen if I give in to this inner strength; it comes from God.

We'll suffer great consequences if we try to achieve the spiritual formation with our own effort, will and strain. God not only implants the desire for transformation into our lives but also supplies the strength to make transformation a reality. Paul is an excellent role model; he demonstrates the balance between grace and training.

Paul lived in the grace of God and at the same time was extraordinary in his personal disciplines. He used an athletic metaphor to describe his life. Athletes subject their physical bodies to harsh disciplines in order to accomplish certain physical goals (1 Corinthians 9:24-27). In reality, we can't separate grace and disciplines; they're deeply intertwined.

The Holy Spirit who endows us with grace is also the Spirit of discipline. The Holy Spirit is the one who empowers us for discipline. He guides us through the disciplines of prayer, fasting, meditation, solitude and self-control.

Jesus was led by the Holy Spirit to fast for forty days in the wilderness. He put his very life in the hands of the Holy Spirit while he lived in this world. Only by the Holy Spirit can we receive the strength to engage in spiritual disciplines.

Followers of Jesus Christ are supposed to be disciplined people. They're supposed to discipline themselves under the grace of God.

PART FOUR

Wilderness—A Preparation

17

God Makes Us Servants
in the Wilderness

🌿

Where does God develop a servant? In the wilderness. Yes, as the Bible reveals, God enrolls his servants in the rough-and-tumble school of the wilderness. One of its best-known alumni is Moses. He had an impressive formal education in the private schools of Egypt, but even at forty years old he wasn't ready to be used by God. Stephen confirmed this: "Moses was instructed in all the wisdom of the Egyptians and was powerful in his words and deeds" (Acts 7:22).

Josephus, a Jewish historian in the first century of the Christian era, wrote much the same thing. Moses had outstanding leadership skills in the palace and performed heroic acts on the battlefield. He even tried to shield his people from the brutality of the Egyptians.

When Moses saw an Egyptian brutally beating a Jew, he made short work of him; that is to say, he killed him, even though it violated both Egyptian and Jewish law when he did so (Exodus 2:11-12). God could have called Moses during this time, but he chose not to.

Instead, God drove the overconfident hero out into the wilderness for some basic training in the Midian desert. After forty years of it, God was then able to call him "a man of God" (Deuteronomy 33:1). Before that, he was known only as "a son of Pharaoh's daughter."

A man or woman of God isn't made in palaces, in comfortable classrooms or quiet dormitories. Sailors get their training on rough seas; soldiers, on rugged terrain. In the same way men and women of God get their spiritual training in the wilderness.

Make no mistake about it, the wilderness is lonely and dangerous, a parched piece of land, crawling with snakes and scorpions (Deuteronomy 8:15). Jeremiah wrote, "They did not say, 'Where is the LORD who brought us up from the land of Egypt, who led us in the wilderness, in a land of deserts and pits, a land of drought and deep darkness, in a land that no one passes through, where no one lives?' " (Jeremiah 2:6).

Why does God drive his people into deserts? He wants to train them as his ministers that they may be well equipped and prepared for all emergencies. What we learn there is not just information or knowledge, skills or techniques. We don't just sharpen our communication skills to gain quick success, sudden fame, flashy prizes. There's far more to learn from the desert.

In the desert those who have trusted only in themselves and others learn to put their faith in God. The Word of God and the Holy Spirit are the teachers. Yes, the curriculum is devoted to suffering, but that's where the lambs become lions. That's where ordinary people become extraordinary men and women of God.

So we shouldn't flee from the desert. Rather we should run toward its unfriendly sands. We shouldn't be afraid of life in the desert; we should embrace it wholeheartedly.

18

Training by Anticipation

✿

One way we are trained in the desert is by waiting.

Moses was impatient. He had a hard time waiting for God. He thought that God would use him when he reached forty, but God had another plan. He didn't call Moses until he was eighty. God's timing is often much slower than our own.

Oswald Chambers, Scottish Bible teacher at the turn of the twentieth century, has said much the same thing: "I want you to ponder on how placid God is! He never rushes into actions." We hurry but God does not. No matter how long it takes, God will always fulfill his promises. He always completes what he sets out to do.

Many great figures of the Bible went through long periods of waiting before God sent them into action. They were restless while God was molding them, but eventually their spirituality matured.

So it is with us. God is more concerned with who we are than who we think we are. He doesn't care how many tasks we do or how big they are. What matters is that we become what God wants us to be. Until that time God won't take delight in our activities. Our efforts at ministry will remain so much huffing and puffing. As Henry Martyn, a missionary to India a century ago, has said, "Teach me that the greatest ministries that I can engage in in this life is to sanctify my soul."

Training in the "school of the desert" is never easy. Waiting, though it seems harmless enough, has its own kind of pain. The forty seemingly insignificant years that Moses spent in the desert were hard years. The most challenging thing he had to suffer was the silence of God. Not only was Moses lonely for human relationships, but he did not even have close fellowship with God.

Joseph lived as a slave and prisoner in Egypt for fourteen years; many times he must have wondered if his dreams had come to an end. When David fled from Saul to save his life, he also went through the terrible pain of waiting. He didn't realize his promised status as king until he was thirty years old.

In the school of waiting, servants of God behave differently than others do. Some are tempted to complain about time wasted, but they resist; instead they use their time to pray and plan and fuel their dreams for the future.

And God is at work while they are waiting.

Joseph adapted to and learned Egyptian culture and language while waiting. To equip him to be prime minister of Egypt, God had to develop his character as well as his talents. David learned to be a humble king while he waited for his time to come. During that waiting period, God had a chance to form in David a wonderful character that allowed him to embrace even his own enemies.

While a servant of God waits, he or she has a chance to anticipate and look forward to what God has planned. Meanwhile, God prepares a platform on which his servant will be able to carry out the intended ministry. While Moses waited in the desert, God removed those who sought his life (Exodus 4:19). God prepared ten plagues and made a way for two million Israelites to leave the slavery of Egypt.

A waiting moment will never be a wasted moment.

19

Discerning God's Time Frame

Every spiritual leader needs discernment about God's time.

The Bible speaks clearly about this talent, which is one of the fruits of desert education. In Issachar, one of the twelve tribes of Israel, there were "those who had understanding of the times, to know what Israel ought to do, two hundred chiefs, and all their kindred under their command" (1 Chronicles 12:32). According to the biblical writer, to understand the signs of the times meant to understand one's era and culture.

God uses those who can understand the times. Moses was one such person. God drove him to the wilderness and sharpened his skills of discernment with regard to the times.

Stephen spoke of this in the book of Acts: "When forty years had passed, an angel appeared to [Moses] in the wilderness of Mount Sinai, in the flame of a burning bush" (Acts 7:30). God developed Moses for the next forty years and finally called him into service at the age of eighty. God moves according to his timeline, not ours.

When we ignore God's timing, the consequences may be severe.

God made a promise to Abraham who was seventy-five years old at the time, but God made him wait twenty-five years before he fulfilled it. The promise was that a son would be born to him and

Sarah. But the aged couple wasn't patient enough to wait for God's precise timing.

Instead, they took matters into their own hands. Using Hagar as a surrogate mother, they had a son of their own, Ishmael. But there was an unintended consequence. For the next thirteen years God did not so much as say a word to Abraham. Yes, when Abraham tried to shorten God's timeline, he made a terrible mistake.

An impatient person is unwilling to wait upon God. That is why God trained Moses in the wilderness. He tamed the wildness in Moses into the gentleness of a servant of God. This virtue isn't inherited as we come to this world, but comes as the fruit of the Spirit.

Picture a strong, wild horse brought into captivity. After some whipping and a lot of whispering, the horse becomes docile and will do what it is told. Like that wild horse, now gentle, the extreme character of Moses became gentle as he waited upon God. As we find in the book of Numbers, "the man Moses was very humble, more so than anyone else on the face of the earth" (Numbers 12:3).

Servants of God must discern God's timing. We should neither act nor move before God's time. Hard, yes. But even Jesus submitted to the timing of the Father. As a result he frequently reminded people, "My hour has not yet come" (John 2:4) or "my time has not yet come" (John 7:6). Before even mentioning the cross, he waited three years. His first mention came after he heard a confession from Peter in Caesarea Philippi (Matthew 16:13-21).

Jesus understood the importance of timing; he knew what to teach his disciples and when to do it.

One distinguishing characteristic of those who are spiritually trained in the desert is their willingness to move only on God's timeline, to respond only to God's voice.

20

Discipline of Solitude

The school of solitude is lonely. If we want a deep-rooted spirituality, however, we have no choice but to enroll in the course called "Loneliness." To become a servant of God requires advanced study in how God uses loneliness; that's to say, how he helps his servants to reach spiritual maturity.

Moses, John the Baptist, Paul. All had to fulfill this requirement. J. Oswald Sanders notes in *Spiritual Leadership* that A. W. Tozer, a renowned preacher and devotional writer of the twentieth century, said, "Most of the world's greatest souls have been lonely. . . . Loneliness seems to be the price a saint must pay for his saintliness."

Why does God put his servants into such awful predicaments? Why does he leave them in such lonely spaces? Because that's where we meet God on his terms. The place where Moses met God wasn't a sparkling Egyptian palace but a dull and desolate wilderness. That's where we find God, and that's where we find ourselves.

Times of quiet and personal reflection are a splendid blessing. We're forced to look deeply into our own lives. But those who don't take advantage of the opportunity are making a mistake.

Henri Nouwen, a Catholic priest and spiritual writer, made a clear distinction between loneliness and solitude. In his book *Reaching Out* he connected loneliness to the desert life and solitude to "the garden." In other words, the desert of our loneliness can be converted into a garden of solitude only by gentle, persistent efforts.

Solitude isn't just being alone. Solitude is being alone with God. Loneliness isn't meant just to cause pain but to lead us deeper into fellowship with God. It's no wonder then that for Nouwen the movement from loneliness to solitude was "the beginning of any spiritual life."

We need to make time to be alone with God. What a blessing that time can be!

We shouldn't be afraid to be alone. A. W. Tozer sums it up this way. "A big eagle flies alone. A big lion hunts alone. Great men of God walk alone." God seeks those who like to be alone with him.

Being alone should never be our main goal. The purpose of being alone is to be equipped to be with others. My favorite spiritual author, Richard Foster, quotes Dietrich Bonhoeffer in *Celebration of Discipline* to the same effect.

"Let him who cannot be alone beware of community. . . . Let him who is not in community beware of being alone." And he [Bonhoeffer] continues to say that "Each by itself has profound pitfalls and perils. One who wants fellowship without solitude plunges into the void of words and feelings, and one who seeks solitude without fellowship perishes in the abyss of vanity, self-infatuation, and despair."

In all our spiritual living we need balance. We must be alone in order to be with others, and we must be with others in order to be alone. Although most of us won't have to spend time in an actual desert, as Moses did, we must remember that the wilderness spiritual writers talk of isn't a physical but a spiritual space.

Sometimes, we have no choice but to be alone.

When we undergo internal struggles, God wants to meet us where we are.

21

Discipline of Hearing God

❧

The wilderness is a perfect spot for hearing the voice of God. That's where Moses heard it, in the desert of Midian. We servants of God have to follow his example. Servants of God aren't controlled by what they hear from fellow human beings; they are controlled by the voice of God.

Moses mingled with so many people in the Egyptian palace and heard so much that he couldn't hear himself think. No wonder he couldn't hear God's voice. As a victorious military leader, he regularly heard people chanting "Moses! Moses! Moses!" But the chanters drowned out the voice of God.

So what else could God do but move Moses to the wilderness? Moses heard his voice and wanted to speak. And the rest is spiritual history.

Wilderness and *word*—both share the same origin in the Hebrew language. God's word called Moses to the wilderness. Deuteronomy put it this way: "[God] sustained him in a desert land, in a howling wilderness waste; he shielded him, cared for him, guarded him as the apple of his eye" (Deuteronomy 32:10). God says that he finds his people in desert land.

Servants of God find their purpose in life by listening to the voice of God. In his book *The Root of the Righteous*, A. W. Tozer gave this advice: "Listen to no man who fails to listen to God." Tozer had no use for those who spoke the Word of God to others before they heard it first themselves.

"We must hear worthily," wrote Tozer elsewhere in the book. If we have ears to hear, we can hear God whenever and wherever we might be. As Tozer explained, Peter was brought to repentance "by the crowing of a rooster." Augustine was brought to repentance "by seeing a friend killed by lightning." Nicolas Herman [Brother Lawrence of the Resurrection] was converted "through seeing a tree stripped of its leaves in winter."

To be a servant of God we must sharpen our hearing. That's what Moses had to do in the wilderness. Our hearing will improve as we go through the wilderness experience. The voice of God becomes clearer.

In his book *The Problem of Pain*, C. S. Lewis put it this way. "The human spirit will not even begin to try to surrender self-will as long as all seems to be well with it. . . . God whispers to us in our pleasures, speaks in our conscience, but shouts in our pains: it is his megaphone to rouse a deaf world." Yes, pain can be a blessing; it helps us to hear God.

The voice of God is a voice of love. We want to hear God's voice, and God wants to hear ours. According to twentieth-century Protestant theologian Paul Tillich, quoted by Alan Loy McGinnis in *The Friendship Factor,* "The first duty of love is to listen." Our love matures as we listen. The wilderness can be a beautiful place when we start to hear God. As we learn to listen, desert flowers bloom and the wilderness is filled with love.

For Jesus the wilderness was a garden where he went to speak

with God, and where God spoke to him. In a sense, writes Henri
Nouwen in *Making All Things New,* "All of Jesus's body functioned
as ears." That's to say, when it came to listening to God, he was all
ears. He heard the voice of God and followed it.

22

Discipline of
Prayer and the Word

❧

Prayer and the Word are two important pillars of spiritual discipline. God trained Moses in both.

The Bible doesn't show Moses praying before he went to the wilderness. It was only after he went to the deserts and mountains and enrolled in the school of the wilderness that he became a man of prayer. And from his prayer life came his spiritual leadership.

Moses dealt with all his problems through prayer. When he had to battle Pharaoh, he knelt before God in prayer and experienced deliverance. Even Pharaoh knew that Moses was a man of prayer. When the Egyptians were suffering from swarming flies, he asked Moses to pray for him (Exodus 8:28).

Prayer was also a way for Moses to hear God. When he faced the Red Sea and there was no place left to hide, he prayed. At the bitter water of Marah, he prayed. But what did the Israelites do while he prayed? Often they grumbled and complained (Exodus 15:23-25).

In Exodus Moses raised his two hands in prayer while the Israelites did battle with the Amalekites (Exodus 17:8-11). As long as

Moses held his ground and prayed, the Israelites received blessings from God.

In Exodus Moses prayed and received the word from God on a mountain for forty days (Exodus 24:18). In their ignorance the people of Israel refused to wait on the Lord; instead they built a golden calf. What a contrast!

Moses shows us that prayer time is never wasted time. Quite the contrary, it is a time full of blessing, a time of spiritual victory. The lesson is quite clear. Before trying to move the hearts of other people, we should try to move the heart of God.

During his stay at the wilderness, Moses also was trained in the Word. He met God at Mount Sinai; he ate what God provided; he prayed and received the Word. The point is hard to miss. The people of God should eat and live by the Word of God.

In Egypt the Israelites ate Egyptian food; they also drank water from the Nile River. In the wilderness they ate manna from heaven (Exodus 16:35) and drank water from a rock (Exodus 17:6).

Each day for forty years God provided exactly enough manna for the people. It was collected and apportioned to the people; what was left uneaten didn't last more than a day, except on the day before the sabbath, when it lasted two days. The lesson is obvious. God demanded complete obedience from his people then as he does now.

God could have rained manna upon his people anytime during the night or day, but he chose to do so early in the morning. This gives us a clue about the way God trains his people. Servants of God should pray early in the morning and consume the Word of God as it falls.

Psalm 46:5 tells us, "God is in the midst of the city; it shall not be moved; / God will help it when the morning dawns." God wants to meet with his people before daybreak. Here we must follow the example of Moses.

As the Israelites fixed their eyes on the sky, so early in the morning we must also look upward. We too need to feed on the Word of God. The crops of the earth are good, but better still are the things that come from heaven, like prayer and the Word of God. These are the things that the apostles made the greatest priorities in their lives (Acts 6:4).

In conclusion, the wilderness is a place where earth and heaven come together, and where God and people join their joyful hands.

23

Discipline of Self-Shattering

❧

God breaks his servants in the wilderness, but he won't completely shatter them. The hand of God is skillful and precise. His hand is tender and delicate.

The prophet Isaiah put it this way. "We are the clay, and you are our potter; / we are all the work of your hand" (Isaiah 64:8).

The prophet Malachi put it another way:

Who can endure the day of his coming, and who can stand when he appears? . . .

For he is like a refiner's fire and like fullers' soap; he will sit as a refiner and purifier of silver, and he will purify the descendants of Levi and refine them like gold and silver, until they present offerings to the LORD in righteousness. (Malachi 3:2-3)

God won't consider using someone who trusts only in himself. Overconfidence in self will always be a stumbling block to one who desires to serve God. Moses is a good example of this.

He had faith in himself when he was forty years old. He trusted in himself to accomplish the work of God. He led the Israelites with his own strength. Yes, but with his physical strength he was able to strangle to death only one Egyptian.

God knew that Moses put too much trust in his own vigor. To accomplish the great task that he had in mind, he had to send Moses into the desert, where he waited until Moses cried out "Enough!" In Exodus 3 Moses confessed to God that he could not carry out what God wanted to accomplish through him. From that moment on, he learned to live and work with God.

Our own meager strength isn't enough to do the work God wants. The great tasks are possible only through his power. Moses found that out when he came into the presence of God in the burning bush. After that he became the great leader of two million people. He stood before the roaring Red Sea and proclaimed, "Do not be afraid, stand firm, and see the deliverance that the LORD will accomplish for you today; for the Egyptians whom you see today you shall never see again" (Exodus 14:13).

After crossing the Red Sea, Moses and the children of Israel were able to sing

The LORD is my strength and my might,
   and he has become my salvation;
this is my God, and I will praise him,
   my father's God, and I will exalt him. (Exodus 15:2)

Yes, God can use anyone in ministry as long as that person doesn't have a stubborn will. The hard-hearted he drives into the harsh desert.

Remember, seeds of wheat must die first before they can become part of the harvest. Living water comes through the shattered stone. The saving blood of Jesus flows from his broken body.

Yes, brokenness, as bad as it is, does bring forth blessings and glory.

24

Discipline of Self-Denial

Those who enroll in the school of the wilderness must begin with the discipline of self-denial. Sadly, self-denial is often confused with self-contempt, extreme abasement, loss of personal identity or despising oneself. But in the Bible it means something quite different. It means trading in one's earthly identity for one's true identity in Christ.

When Jesus lived in this world, he had a firm knowledge of who he was. Yet in the interrogations leading up to his death he said little or nothing to the interrogators; dragging his cross at the end, he was like a lamb being led to slaughter.

However, during his vigorous life on this earth, when someone asked who he was, he didn't hesitate to answer. "Have I been with you all this time, Philip, and you still do not know me? Whoever has seen me has seen the Father. How can you say, 'Show us the Father'?" (John 14:9).

Jesus understood himself as Messiah, as King of kings, as God. He held onto his true identity while he was on this earth, but what he did relinquish were some of his rights. Although he never ceased to be God, he didn't consider equality with God a thing to be exploited (Philippians 2:6).

[He] emptied himself,
    taking the form of a slave,
    being born in human likeness.
And being found in human form,
    he humbled himself
    and became obedient to the point of death—
    even death on a cross. (Philippians 2:7-8)

It isn't easy for someone who knows his or her own tremendous value to relinquish self-identity. Moses knew who he was; he had lived in the Egyptian palace and received a splendid education as part of the royal family. He built his body into excellent condition. He knew how to control his temper.

To earn such high degree of education, leadership skill and eloquence, he had to practice a rigorous disciplined life.

He knew exactly who he was and what he had to do. He was a great person destined to do great things. "He supposed that his kinsfolk would understand that God through him was rescuing them" (Acts 7:25). However, God had a different plan for how that calling would be carried out. It would begin by his denying his own identity and finding his true identity in God. And so it is with us. The power of God becomes a reality in our lives when we deny our nature; this is a basic principle of ministry.

On this very point, speaking to his disciples and the crowd around him, Jesus said, "If any want to become my followers, let them deny themselves and take up their cross and follow me" (Mark 8:34).

Yes, following Jesus means denying ourselves every day. By relinquishing our own selves, we fulfill the will of God.

25

Discipline of Shepherding

Moses worked as a shepherd during his stay in the desert of Midian. As Exodus records, "Moses was keeping the flock of his father-in-law Jethro, the priest of Midian; he led his flock beyond the wilderness, and came to Horeb, the mountain of God" (Exodus 3:1).

Why did God send Moses to do such a thing? Because there's a very close parallel between taking care of sheep and taking care of Israelites.

David, a man after God's own heart, was also a shepherd. In one of his psalms he says:

> He chose his servant David,
> and took him from the sheepfolds;
> from tending the nursing ewes he brought him
> to be the shepherd of his people Jacob,
> of Israel, his inheritance.
> With upright heart he tended them,
> and guided them with skillful hand. (Psalm 78:70-72)

Moses had once killed an Egyptian without thinking twice about it and would do it again if the situation presented itself. For this reason God made Moses tend sheep in the desert; there he learned the importance of each and every sheep. As Jesus said, a good shepherd gives his life for his sheep. This was the kind of training Moses had to go through before he was ready to lead the children of Israel.

During the time of the Exodus, God was prepared to destroy the Israelites when they disobeyed him. In that critical moment Moses prayed that God would forgive them; if not, he said to the Lord, "blot me out of the book that you have written" (Exodus 32:32). It was the good shepherd who knew the value of each member of his flock.

David's story is similar. God wanted to make him a king, but first he sent him on a trial, to take care of lambs. As the Bible records, "David said to Saul, 'Your servant used to keep sheep for his father; and whenever a lion or a bear came, and took a lamb from the flock, I went after it and struck it down, rescuing the lamb from its mouth; and if it turned against me, I would catch it by the jaw, strike it down, and kill it' " (1 Samuel 17:34-35). Then, after watching David mature as a shepherd, God chose him as a leader of his people.

Servants of God should assign value and meaning even to the smallest tasks. As Jesus said, "Whoever is faithful in a very little is faithful also in much; and whoever is dishonest in a very little is dishonest also in much" (Luke 16:10).

Jesus said much the same thing in the parable of the talents: "Well done, good and trustworthy slave; you have been trustworthy in a few things, I will put you in charge of many things; enter into the joy of your master" (Matthew 25:23).

The desert is where we all are trained to serve in small matters. There the servants of God learn to have a heart like Jesus. Jesus is the one who searches for a lost sheep (Luke 15:4). It is Jesus who gave up his life for the sake of his sheep. It is in the desert that we servants of God learn to become good shepherds too.

26

Discipline of Serving

✣

Did the heart of Moses really change in the desert? Apparently, yes.

As the book of Exodus records, some shepherds raided the flocks of the daughters of the priest of Midian. "Moses got up and came to their defense and watered their flock" (Exodus 2:17).

When Moses lived in the palace of Egypt, he had servants to see to his every need, but in the desert he was just another anonymous shepherd tending flocks of sheep. Alone and afraid, he got down on his knees, praying and shedding tears for his sins and those of the Israelites. Yes, Christian leadership rises from bended knees, tearful eyes and broken hearts.

Those who uphold the kingdom of God have to become servants. That is what Jesus did, making himself nothing and taking on the nature of a servant. As he once put it, "The Son of Man came not to be served but to serve, and to give his life a ransom for many" (Mark 10:45).

This aspect of Jesus's character also surfaces in John 13. Wrapping a towel around himself and picking up a basin, he washed his disciples' feet. What a precious picture of Jesus the servant!

Human beings love to be served. Most of us would much rather be served by others than to serve others. Jesus' disciples were no exception. They "began to be angry with James and John" when they heard that the lads had asked Jesus to let them sit on each side of him in this world and the next.

In reality, all twelve disciples wanted the same thing. To these Jesus gave a sharp rebuke. "Whoever wishes to become great among you must be your servant, and whoever wishes to be first among you must be slave of all" (Mark 10:43-44).

In order to be great in God's kingdom, we must learn to serve others. But we'll never serve others until we learn to deny ourselves. All servants of God must put aside their own selfish desires in order to serve their neighbors. Unless we forgive our neighbors' faults and negligences, we can't truly serve them.

To be a servant to our neighbors, we must deny ourselves and even treat the enemies next door like people we are meeting for the first time. As we renew our lives every day, we also need to make our hearts new toward our neighbors. Only then can we can serve them without bitterness and remorse.

How then can we serve others? Start with small things first. Human beings that we are, the first thing that always comes to mind is the big thing, the gigantic thing. God, however, puts more emphasis on smaller things. Jesus put it in an unforgettable way: "Just as you did it to one of the least of these who are members of my family, you did it to me" (Matthew 25:40).

27

The Wilderness School
of the Holy Spirit

In the school of wilderness, servants of God experience the work of the Holy Spirit. This is yet another reason why the wilderness is a blessed place.

Anointing by the Holy Spirit is closely related to the wilderness experience. Some receive it before they enter the wilderness; others, during or after their wilderness time.

Moses received anointing on his first visit to the wilderness when he found himself facing a burning bush (Exodus 3). That incident was a turning point. Then he went through a huge transformation; his vision, his way of life, his ministries—everything changed. He became at once a man of great wonder and power, and a meek servant of God.

His assistant Joshua received a special anointing of the Holy Spirit. That was after he went through forty years of training in the wilderness (Deuteronomy 34:9).

David was anointed before he enrolled in that hard school of preparation. The Bible says, "Samuel took the horn of oil, and anointed [David] in the presence of his brothers; and the spirit of the LORD came mightily upon David from that day forward" (1 Samuel 16:13). That day became a glorious and gracious day for David. However, he had to run away from Saul and eventually found himself in the wilderness.

Jesus received baptism from John the Baptist and then was led by the Holy Spirit to enter the desert (Matthew 4:1).

Paul met and received that special anointing from Jesus on the road to Damascus (Acts 9), but he eventually ended up in the Arabian Desert (Galatians 1:15-17).

Those who are especially chosen by God have one common experience, a special anointing by the Holy Spirit. That anointing gives neither overnight success nor fame. But rather it leads first of all to the desert. In that desolate place, the worldly self dies, but willing believers are renewed by the Holy Spirit. They no longer belong to the world but became "servants of God."

When the Holy Spirit comes into the wilderness, his presence turns that place into a place of blessing. As the prophet Isaiah writes, "A spirit from on high is poured out on us, and the wilderness becomes a fruitful field, and the fruitful field is deemed a forest" (Isaiah 32:15).

When the Holy Spirit is manifest, the wilderness will be transformed; it will no longer be an arid and parched land but a beautiful place of abundant blessing.

According to Isaiah, when the Holy Spirit comes

The wilderness and the dry land shall be glad,
the desert shall rejoice and blossom;
like the crocus, it shall blossom abundantly,
and rejoice with joy and singing.
The glory of Lebanon shall be given to it,

the majesty of Carmel and Sharon.

They shall see the glory of the LORD,

the majesty of our God. (Isaiah 35:1-2)

The wilderness is a place where God blesses and trains his people (Deuteronomy 8:16). The difficulty of the desert life is meant to lead to an attitude of thanksgiving and gratitude. David confessed, "It is good for me that I was humbled, / so that I might learn your statutes" (Psalm 119:71). Even Charles Colson, the White House counsel who went to jail because of his role in the Watergate scandal, compares his experience in a prison cell to a wilderness school where he learned valuable lessons. As he described it in his book *Loving God*, "Victories come through defeats, healing through brokenness; finding self through losing self."

The school of wilderness, as owned and operated by the Holy Spirit, has never been a comforting place. We all face suffering, confusion, shattering, failure and self-abandonment. But that's where servants of God are made. They all go through transformation, and on the other side find themselves persons of prayer, the Word and the Holy Spirit.

We all need to thank God for giving us the wilderness. It's a blessing in disguise.

PART FIVE

Soul Caring

28

Take a Step Back for Soul Care

🌿

During his earthly life Jesus had seemingly endless resources of passion and strength. Where did they come from? From his solitary time with God.

Luke explains how Jesus kept his life in balance. "Word about Jesus spread abroad; many crowds would gather to hear him and to be cured of their diseases. But he would withdraw to deserted places and pray" (Luke 5:15-16).

Jesus never let the crowd dictate his actions. He pursued his own life rhythms. He preached when he wanted to and went apart to pray when he wanted to. As a minister of God, I have to ask myself whether I have these same rhythms.

Seeing crowds of people coming together to seek Jesus gives me great joy. Meeting people and influencing them gives me great satisfaction. But does this business, this busyness, mean I'm a successful pastor? Maybe it does, but maybe it doesn't. It may indicate that I have a problem. And it isn't just my problem, but that of many who want to serve God at this time in world history.

Servants of God who don't take time off become exhausted. Their power and spiritual resources are drained. Popular ministries may have short lives. World-renowned leaders may burn out because they don't spend time alone with God. The most important task for true servants of God is to take time off to look at one's inner life, to care for one's own soul.

This issue reminds me of Aesop's *Fables*, particularly the one about the goose that laid the golden eggs. As I read it, the golden eggs are less important than the goose that lays them. Without the goose, there would be no more golden eggs!

What has this story got to do with ministry? When a minister abuses his or her strength, then he or she can't produce the golden results. The moral? The minister is more important than the ministry.

Do we want golden results in our ministries? If the answer to that question is yes, then we need to have balanced relationships with others. Consider this piece of wisdom from Paul Reese, missionary and statesman with World Vision, who is quoted by Gail MacDonald in *High Call, High Privilege:* "Learn the rhythm of engaging and disengaging as our Lord did."

Caring for our soul means taking a step back to have a deeper relationship with God. When our hearts grow cold and exhaustion creeps in, the solution doesn't lie in the outer world. It lies in the inner world, where we should rekindle the spiritual fire. Gail MacDonald notes in her book *Of the Imitation of Christ: Selections* that, some centuries ago, Thomas à Kempis, an Augustinian monk who is remembered for his book *The Imitation of Christ*, issued the following warning: "When a man's fervor tapers off, he finds little joy in labor and seeks his consolation elsewhere."

Taking a step back, spending some time together with our Creator, is a small but critical move. If we don't take it now, then we may soon have to retire from the field completely.

Retreating to a quiet place every day will keep us from taking an extended sabbatical.

Balance is the main thing, a harmony of stepping back and coming forward that can make us fruitful and effective in the Spirit.

29

Fine-Tune the Soul
Through Quiet

🌿

Joshua had a habit of rising early in the morning (Joshua 3:1; 7:16; 8:10) and used the time for prayer.

David described the same practice in one of his psalms.

My heart is steadfast, O God,
my heart is steadfast.
I will sing and make melody.
Awake, my soul!
Awake, O harp and lyre!
I will awake the dawn. (Psalm 57:7-8)

And Jesus prayed early in the morning, while it was still dark (Mark 1:35).

Why have so many servants of God before and since Jesus' time thought of morning as precious? To this day they meet God early in the morning to pray, to fine-tune their souls.

Violinists tune their violins with the piano before they perform. The strings should be neither too tight nor too loose. With just the right tension, they make wonderful music.

And there's another resemblance. Like instruments, well-tuned servants of God give peace and comfort to those who hear them. They give glory to God.

Once I forgot to have my piano tuned. It should have been serviced every six months, but I had let the date pass. To get the piano completely back in tune I had to pay the technician to come not once but several times. The moral? Like the soul, the piano should be tuned regularly, lovingly.

This same principle applies to our ministries. Overwork would seem to make them more effective, but often the result is just the opposite. The well-tuned instrument gets off-key, and the strings begin to sag. Of course, we could wait for one grand tune-up, but the longer we wait, the more damage is done. All of which means, to keep in top spiritual condition, our souls need daily devotional time. No one has had a busier, more crowded life than Jesus. But even he made time for his devotions.

Hudson Taylor, a pioneer missionary to China, is a good example. Taylor, whose story is told in Man-Je Cho's book *People Who Can Make the Spare Time Operate the Whole World,* arrived in that land at age twenty-five and lived the rest of his life there. No wonder people asked him the inevitable question: "How could you live all your life as a missionary in a foreign land? What was your secret?" This was his answer: "My dedication and happiness all depended on how I started my days. . . . As I awake in the morning, I start my days making God's will part of mine. When I do that, I find peace and happiness."

We too should keep our souls in tune with God the way musicians tune their instruments.

Early morning devotions help us tune our will to God.

30

Soul Enrichment

One of the obstacles to our spiritual growth is noise. Beware of noise from the outer world. Also guard against the noise that builds up within.

Where does this inner noise come from? Inner noise stems from worry about worldly things. Worldly things produce what is contrary to God (Romans 8:5-6).

The discipline of silence can still the noise of the world. It can turn us from worldly matters to spiritual ones. It is really a form of repentance.

How do our souls grow? Our souls thrive on silence. When does our spirituality build a deeper root system? When we make space for silence. Our souls are enriched by silence; in the quiet they revel and grow.

Take a look at the natural world and you'll see silence at work. Living things grow silently. Trees put down deeper roots without a sound. Trees bear fruit without the slightest noise. In the ocean deep hardly a sound is heard.

Silence is mystical. Silence teaches us. A child in the mother's womb can't make sounds but grows in silence. Early in the morning when we wake to hear nature in silence, we grasp the deeper meaning of our lives.

Silence is a time to dump the garbage from our souls. Oh yes, it's there! And silence helps us admit our sins, encourages us to get rid of them.

Quietly, we confess our sins to God. As Proverbs says, "No one who conceals transgressions will prosper, / but one who confesses and forsakes them will obtain mercy" (Proverbs 28:13).

Silence nourishes meditation on the Word. Our souls grow by digesting the Word. As Matthew says in his Gospel, "One does not live by bread alone, but by every word that comes from the mouth of God" (Matthew 4:4).

Reading the Word is vital to spiritual growth. When we taste the Word, we feed our souls. But for our souls to grow we must digest God's Word. It is the life blood of our souls. It reaches our souls through the discipline of silence.

In silence the Word takes hold in our hearts. It soaks into our hearts through prayer. Then we understand. As spiritual writer Thomas Moore has said in his book *Caring for the Soul*, "Through the discipline of silence, we understand and come near to the truth."

Understanding links all things together. It connects God and self. It links the past and the present, the present and the future, the present and the eternal until we come to see everything from an eternal vantage point.

Silence is a friend of God. Silence is God's gift to deepen our love and friendship. When we talk a lot, love seems to be absent. But when we come together face to face, we sense a mystical feeling of love.

31

Tend the Inner Garden

Caring and cultivating our spiritual world are two closely related concepts. God moves and acts in our hearts. When we cultivate our hearts, we uncover the great blessings God has planted there.

These blessings can truly be called treasures from God. But these treasures aren't decorations like the ones we use to fill our homes.

Our spirits are living; they need care, attention, cultivation. Then they'll bring forth healthier, more gracious results.

We need to care for our hearts because they're ambivalent. Our hearts are corrupted, but still they're our source of life. As Jeremiah said:

> The heart is devious above all else;
> it is perverse—
> who can understand it? (Jeremiah 17:9)

This verse reveals what we already know: our hearts are depraved.

The good and bad in our hearts are constantly in tension. One impulse is toward heaven, the other toward hell. As Solomon said, "Above all else, guard your heart, / for it is the wellspring of life" (Proverbs 4:23 NIV). This verse puts our hearts in a positive light.

Why is guarding the heart so important? Because the words that we speak arise from our hearts. Our hearts also dictate the actions we take. Yes, both speech and action are governed by our hearts.

Jesus himself had the last word on the importance of the heart. "The good person out of the good treasure of the heart produces good, and the evil person out of evil treasure produces evil" (Luke 6:45). With this verse as our guide we know how to cultivate the garden of our hearts.

In the garden of our hearts, we want splendid fruit-bearing trees. But we can't have the trees without having planted the seeds. What does the Bible say about seeds? They are the Word of God (Matthew 13:19).

Meditate and pray, plant the Word, and there will be good and beautiful fruit. What fruit? The fruit of the Spirit! The apostle Paul described the varieties in his letter to the Galatians: "Love, joy, peace, patience, kindness, generosity, faithfulness, gentleness, and self-control" (Galatians 5:22-23). To bear such beautiful fruit we must have a farmer's heart, taking care of our souls every day.

What if weeds grow in the garden of our hearts? Weeds are hard to get rid of; they're stubborn and persistent. They confuse and distort the Word that is sprouting to life. Paul warned us about such weeds:

> The works of the flesh are obvious: fornication, impurity, licentiousness, idolatry, sorcery, enmities, strife, jealousy, anger, quarrels, dissensions, factions, envy, drunkenness, carousing, and things like these. I am warning you, as I warned you before: those who do such things will not inherit the kingdom of God. (Galatians 5:19-21)

What's a weed, and what isn't? How can we get rid of them? Repentance is the answer. Let's rid ourselves of the thoughts that are weeds and bear the fruits of the Holy Spirit!

32

Harmonize the
Inner and Outer Worlds

❧

One of the worst issues for Christians is hypocrisy. Many of us are slaves to this, and we barely know it. The Bible defines it as saying one thing but doing just the opposite. When thoughts and actions don't match up, we try to deceive ourselves and others by our words and actions; we become hypocrites.

The book of Proverbs describes such people:

Like the glaze covering an earthen vessel
are smooth lips with an evil heart.
An enemy dissembles in speaking
while harboring deceit within. (Proverbs 26:23-24)

Jesus condemned such hypocrites as whitewashed tombs. This is a striking way to put it because he was so kind to tax collectors, prostitutes and sinners of all sorts. But Jesus confronted the hypocrites and denounced them publicly: "Woe to you, scribes and Pharisees, hypocrites! For you clean the outside of the cup and of the plate, but inside they are full of greed and self-indulgence" (Matthew 23:25).

Again Jesus said, "You are like whitewashed tombs, which on the outside look beautiful, but inside they are full of the bones of the dead and all kinds of filth" (Matthew 23:27).

Whenever I read and meditate on these verses, I feel that the Lord is reproving me for "holding on to the outward form of godliness but denying its power" (2 Timothy 3:5).

Is it possible to spot godliness in a person we pass on the street? Not according to the Bible. Many of God's favorites had more beauty in their inner life than in their outward appearance.

Saul, the first king of Israel, was "a handsome young man. There was not a man among the people of Israel more handsome than he; he stood head and shoulders above everyone else" (1 Samuel 9:2). But God passed over Saul and chose David. When Samuel looked for David to anoint him, God told him not to look for outer beauty but beauty of the heart.

Among David's sons there was one who had a flawless appearance. "In all Israel there was no one to be praised so much for his beauty as Absalom; from the sole of his foot to the crown of his head there was no blemish in him" (2 Samuel 14:25). But in his heart he fomented revenge against Amnon who violated his sister. Eventually, Absalom murdered Amnon. His personal appearance continued to dazzle; yet in his heart he was a murderer. Yes, he was like a tomb: on the outside the whitewash looked fresh; inside, corruption continued its inevitable task

According to the prophecy of Isaiah, the Messiah would win no beauty contests. He would have "no form or majesty that we should look at him, nothing in his appearance that we should desire him" (Isaiah 53:2). But his inner world would be splendid with such qualities as peace, joy, meekness, mercy and love. When he opened his mouth, gracious words were heard by those who came near to him (Luke 4:22).

Though lacking in his outward appearance, Jesus was inwardly permeated with love. His inner and outer life were in harmony. No matter what other people did to him, he always reacted with good deeds.

Spiritual disciplines will make us more like Jesus; they'll make our lips and heart become one.

Being like Jesus, avoiding hypocrisy, is all about taking care of our souls.

PART SIX

Ways to Fruitfulness

33

What Is God Looking For?

🌿

God didn't tell us to become beautiful flowers. Instead, he commanded us to bear fruit. The fig tree symbolizes the country of Israel, and what is it known for? Bearing fruit.

No doubt the fig tree has a flower; all trees flower before bearing fruit. But why have we rarely heard about flowering fig trees? It's the fruit we value, the figs themselves.

Yes, the fig tree as a symbol of the will of God had something to tell Israel. God did not want just a flowering nation but a fruitful one.

Christ mentions fruit as a sign of discipleship. "My father is glorified by this, that you bear much fruit and become my disciples" (John 15:8). Jesus charged his disciples to imitate the flowering fruit trees. "You did not choose me but I chose you. And I appointed you to go and bear fruit, fruit that will last, so that the Father will give you whatever you ask him in my name" (John 15:16). And so Jesus charges us.

Why do I say we need to be more than beautiful flowers? I know that flowers have a lovely fragrance. But fruit offers something much more precious than flowers. It produces seed, brings life, looks to the future.

Next time you pick up a piece of fruit, count the seeds you find inside. Imagine the countless trees that could spring from them. And yet each tree grows from such a humble and hidden beginning.

Can we open up to this? Can we imagine it? Think what God wants to do with us when he asks us to bear fruit. He wants us to multiply, to make things grow, to give life.

A pretty flower seems to be looking for popularity. Sometimes we are just like them! We want to be the center of attention, to be flattered and admired. Many people aspire to this. Fame is their idea of success. If only they could understand how trivial this dream really is!

Fruit, on the other hand, is modest and serious; it develops quietly, away from the public gaze, preparing for its vital role in the future.

Bearing fruit reveals the good character God wants for his people.

As much as God loves the flower of trees, he isn't interested in flashy bouquets or fancy floral displays. What he values is the inner beauty, the beauty of the heart. Yes, he understands our need for attention. Yes, he dances his attention on us. But what he really wants us to do is to grow, to be substantial, to give life.

We may be flowers for a few brief moments, but we yearn for a more substantial life. God tells us to bear fruit because he wants us to thrive, grow, contribute; to create an orchard, grove, forest. In other words, he wants the future to unfold through us.

What should we do? Don't focus on gaining attention, being famous, finding worldly success. God desires fruitful Christians, not financially successful Christians. God wants Christians who bear witness to his grace in the world.

34

Bear Fruit by
Christlike Descending

❧

Spirituality is all about bearing fruit. Bushels of fruit should be our spiritual goal. But what kind of fruit does God desire?

John the Baptist proclaimed repentance; in preaching, he also spoke of the importance of producing good fruit. "Even now the ax is lying at the root of the trees; every tree therefore that does not bear good fruit is cut down and thrown into the fire" (Luke 3:9). Those who came to John the Baptist were puzzled: "What then should we do?" (v. 10).

John wanted to see their lives transformed. He told them to share their clothes and food with those who had none. That kind of generosity is a way of bearing fruit. What will transform us in this way?

Jesus told a secret about bearing fruit.

"I tell you, unless a grain of wheat falls into the earth and dies, it remains just a single grain; but if it dies, it bears much fruit. Those who love their life will lose it, and those who hate their life in this world will keep it for eternal life" (John 12:24-25).

This understanding of how to bear fruit comes down to us from above. "A grain of wheat falls into the earth." These words speak volumes about the life of Jesus. The life of Jesus is a life that comes down to us. He descended from heaven. He even came down to a manger. His whole life is one of coming down from above.

Worldly authorities strive for the highest positions. They want to be the focus of everyone's attention. Reputation, fame, popularity, cultivating an image—all these are of prime importance for them.

Jesus had the exact opposite point of view. He kept coming down to our level. He served from the lowliest position. He had no interest in exalting his public image. Instead, he took on the image of the little child in the manger. Another image of humility he gave us: that of dying a cruel death on the cross.

Jesus valued God's kingdom above all. But we value our own images far more than the gospel. We consider the reputations of our churches more valuable than the Lord. In that way our spiritualities fall short.

There is a great difference between an ordinary, everyday person and one who condescends to us from the highest place of all. Jesus amazed us because he left the higher realms and came down to our lower depths. That is why his influence was so remarkable. He lived in heaven but came down to serve.

How can Christians follow this example? Can we come down from our own high places to serve others? Only then will we really be following our Lord Jesus. And we'll bear splendid fruit when we do.

As Lao Tzu, ancient Chinese philosopher and founder of Taoism, wrote in his book *Tao Te Ching*, "The sea is the king of a hundred streams because it lies below them." Jesus is like the sea because he serves all the people from the lowest depths although he himself is the king of all kings.

35

Be Fruitful by Putting Self-Interest Aside

Spirituality that bears fruit descends from above and hides its true identity. A grain of wheat has first to come down and die. A seed must first be planted under ground. That is the kind of life Jesus lived.

Patience is what we need till that seed begins to sprout. Working with hidden seed is part of mature spiritual discipline. We must wait to see our disciplines bear fruit.

Some people delight in showing off. Popularity is what they're after. But showing off, swanning around, isn't what Jesus intended. He had a deeper spiritual discipline in mind.

Notice how Jesus tried to conceal his own identity. He wasn't born in an elegant home or to a family of influence. Yes, he had a respectable lineage, but Mary was just a simple woman of her time. Nobody expected much from her, but God hid his life in her.

Bethlehem, where Jesus was born, wasn't a thriving city like Jerusalem, admired by all of Israel. It was a small town. No one there had great expectations, and no one in Jerusalem expected much to come from that peasant town.

What about the town where Jesus spent his early life? "Can anything good come out of Nazareth?" (John 1:46). That is what Nathanael spouted off when he was being recruited by Philip. Later, in Galilee, where Jesus began his active ministry, most of the communities were devoted to agriculture and fishing. Yes, Jesus took the low road, and he was slow to reveal himself.

Whenever Jesus healed the sick, he warned them not to tell a soul. As he said to one leper, "See that you say nothing to anyone; but go, show yourself to the priest" (Mark 1:44).

Did the leper do Jesus the favor of keeping the healing a secret?

"He went out and began to proclaim it freely, and to spread the word, so that Jesus could no longer go into a town openly, but stayed out in the country; and people came to him from every quarter" (Mark 1:45).

After Jesus fed the five thousand with five loaves and two fish, people demanded that he become their king. He refused and went out to a lonely place to pray (John 6:15).

In our own world we often think our greatest task is to let the crowd know how wonderful we are. We measure our own worth only by what others think of us. If we aren't recognized, we get anxious.

We brag about our ministries and puff up our accomplishments. But if we are as good as we think we are, shouldn't we let God do the publicizing?

To offer a helping hand to others is a noble thing, and God will publicize it in his own good time. Self-promotion isn't what pleases God.

Those who feel confident about themselves don't need to boast. Their lives are already full to overflowing.

36

We Shatter Ourselves
to Bear Fruit

The spirituality of Jesus reaches its peak on the cross. He broke his body on the cross to produce abundant fruit of salvation for all humankind. In the Gospel of John, Jesus portrays his life with rich comparisons to seed and fruit (John 12:24-25).

Jesus shows us how a fruit-bearing life descends from above. He also shows us how to conceal one's own life. The peak of this kind of life is abandoning or shattering of self.

A seed that falls to the ground but doesn't die won't produce new life. Only when that seed is broken will the new life begin.

Precious spiritual things are hidden away. Isaiah describes this mystery:

> I will give you the treasures of darkness
>   and riches hidden in secret places,
> so that you may know that it is I, the LORD,
>   the God of Israel, who call you by your name. (Isaiah 45:3)

This life we have from God is our hidden treasure. We who have accepted Jesus have this rich treasure deep within our hearts. It's eternal life; it reveals the character and power of God.

How can we make this hidden life flow into the world? When our walls of self are shattered, this life in us pours out.

What do I mean by shattering of the self? The Bible has different meanings of self. Sometimes the self is a physical body; sometimes, the soul. Sometimes the Bible speaks of the old self and the new self.

But when I say the self must be tamed and broken, I'm speaking of a hardened outer self that limits the life within. When we let ourselves be shattered, we bring God's hidden life into the open.

How can we shatter the outer walls that hold the life of God in check? How can we let the life of God flow free? One way is to deny ourselves. As the Lord said, "If any want to become my followers, let them deny themselves and take up their cross daily and follow me" (Luke 9:23).

Paul discovered that the power of God flowed without limits when his self was broken. "I die every day! That is as certain, brothers and sisters, as my boasting of you—a boast that I make in Christ Jesus our Lord" (1 Corinthians 15:31).

God shattered a rock to let water flow for thirsty Israelites. When Moses hit the rock, water gushed forth. When God struck Jesus the Rock, living water began to flow. The blood and the water he shed on the cross gave life to our souls. His precious blood had the power to cleanse sins. The water pouring from his side was a sign of the Holy Spirit.

After shedding his blood on the cross, Jesus poured living water, the water of the Holy Spirit, on those who were gathered at the feast of Pentecost. From that moment on the Holy Spirit became a sign in preaching of the gospel and has helped to gain the salvation of the world ever since.

We too must experience the brokenness of Jesus. We too must be shattered. Only from that will come the great blessing, abundant fruit.

37

We Are Fruitful Through Close Friendship With God

God longs to have a friendship with us. But he wants more than that. He wants a close friendship. And this is the only way we can bear the fruit God wants.

As Jesus said, "I am the vine, you are the branches. Those who abide in me and I in them bear much fruit, because apart from me you can do nothing" (John 15:5).

Only when we become close friends with Jesus can we produce abundant spiritual fruit. Those who exercise this deeper spirituality have gone beyond pleasing God; they're actually working together with God. Their ministries aren't for God but through God.

Working for God is easy enough, but working with God and through God requires something more. This is a simple distinction but also a profound one. But, sad to say, it can also confound some ministers of God; they can't tell the difference.

God is looking for balance in our friendship and ministry. As Dawson Trotman, founder of The Navigators, has said, "We should never be in a situation where we work so hard to bring the kingdom but do not have much time to spend with God."

Without a close friendship with Jesus, our ministries won't count. Working hard is only the half of it. Friendship is the other half.

Like a living branch on a healthy tree, we receive what we need to grow and bear fruit. The branch is empowered by the life-giving tree.

Jesus knew this principle well. First he called his disciples and became friends of theirs. Then he gave them responsibilities. Mark records this. "He appointed twelve, whom he also named apostles, to be with him, and to be sent out to proclaim the message, and to have authority to cast out demons" (Mark 3:14-15).

To become his ministers we must spend time with Jesus. We get to know his heart, his vision, his concerns and what makes him strong. In our thoughts we meet him. His tears become ours, and his prayer becomes ours.

If we want this close friendship with Jesus, we have to forfeit many things. We have to set aside time to spend with him. We have to kneel in front of him. We have to gaze on him. We have to have identical goals, like-minded will and Christlike hands. That's when we may be said to have a deeper fellowship with him.

In this deeper relationship we'll discover what Jesus wants us to do and how he gives us strength to do it. How can we abide with Jesus? How can we unite with him? When we abide in the Word, we become one (John 8:31); that's to say, Jesus is in the Word, and the Word is in Jesus (John 1:1-3). When we pray with his Word, we're immersed in his life (John 15:7).

Just as a married couple unites to conceive a child, we also will receive a spiritual begetting when we become friends with Jesus.

In this friendship we enter into the salvation of the world.

PART SEVEN

Righteousness Has a Heart

38

A Vessel for the
Power of God

&

God looks for something special in his ministers. He wants them to accomplish many and varied tasks, but to do them they must all have one thing in common. Purity.

Paul explained it this way in his second letter to Timothy: "All who cleanse themselves of the things I have mentioned will become special utensils, dedicated and useful to the owner of the house, ready for every good work" (2 Timothy 2:21). That's to say, what God expects a servant to be is a pure, clean, cool instrument; not necessarily a sledge hammer, but a sanitized, sterilized, efficient instrument.

What kind of instrument was Jesus? He came into the world as an insignificant figure; he wasn't a person of great influence. Born in a manger, raised in humble circumstances, he didn't achieve what we usually call success. He died on the cross like a common thief.

Isaiah described the Messiah this way:

He grew up . . . like a young plant,
    and like a root out of dry ground;

he had no form or majesty that we should look at him,
nothing in his appearance that we should desire him.
(Isaiah 53:2)

But Jesus had God's power within; he was God's instrument.

Jesus often spoke about the power of God. Divine power often flowed from him. "All in the crowd were trying to touch him, for power came out from him and healed all of them" (Luke 6:19).

One of the crowd, a woman who was suffering from a continual flow of blood, approached him, and he cried out, "Someone touched me; for I noticed that power had gone out from me" (Luke 8:46). And so she was healed.

Yes, with the power of the Holy Spirit, Jesus cast out evil spirits, but he preferred to remain obscure; he didn't want to be recognized for the wrong reason. In that way he was a spiritually effective instrument, not a flashy one.

What kind of person does God work through? Not a person who boasts about his or her competence. Instead, God looks for someone who maintains power inwardly. As Hudson Taylor, missionary to China, said, "God uses those who are utterly weak enough to trust him only."

Spiritual discipline is about keeping the instrument pure and simple.

Spiritual discipline is about denying ourself.

Spiritual discipline is about losing our edge in this world, only to regain the spiritual edge when God does the sharpening.

39

Deeper Spirituality and Pain

God sets a great value on those who endure great trials. He purifies his servants through suffering and readies them for his ministries.

God's guidelines are different from those the world uses, as Paul told the Corinthians. "Consider your own call, brothers and sisters: not many of you were wise by human standards, not many were powerful, not many were of noble birth" (1 Corinthians 1:26).

God does choose the intelligent and the noble from time to time, but he prefers those who are neglected by the world. After he makes his choice, he molds each person through suffering into deeper spiritual formation.

Jesus was without sin, but no exception was made for him; he too was formed by suffering. The author of Hebrews offers this explanation: "Although he was a Son, he learned obedience through what he suffered; and having been made perfect, he became the source of eternal salvation for all who obey him" (Hebrews 5:8-9). Suffering was a tool to develop the deeper spirituality of Jesus.

Servants of God are purified through suffering. "Take away the dross from the silver, / and the smith has material for a vessel" (Proverbs 25:4). To remove dross, the silver must be put into the fire. The silversmith's furnace symbolizes suffering. In that enormous heat the dross is burned away, and what's left is the silver, pure and simple.

Consider Job. He was a man who had everything. He was rich both in prosperity and in righteousness, and he was blessed with children. But before God could give him a mission, he had to go through a trial. Job understood this: "He knows the way that I take; / when he has tested me, I shall come out like gold" (Job 23:10).

God called Paul—he was named Saul then—to convey a message to the Gentiles. It wasn't a gentle call but a rough one on the road to Damascus. God also called the priest Ananias who didn't want to minister to this enemy of God. "But the Lord said to him, 'Go, for he is an instrument whom I have chosen to bring my name before Gentiles and kings and before the people of Israel; I myself will show him how much he must suffer for the sake of my name'" (Acts 9:15-16).

Yes, Paul found that he had much to undergo and endure. His life story became one of suffering. The weaker he got, the deeper his spirituality became. And the deeper it got, the more he became like Christ. The more Christlike he became, the more effective he became in spreading the news about the Messiah

What's the moral? Like Paul, we should see in our own trials and tribulations an opportunity to grow.

40

Righteousness Has a Heart

Holiness is having a heart for God, but even the holiest among us have doubts from time to time. But doubting has its limits, as the letter of James reminds us: "The doubter, being double-minded and unstable in every way, must not expect to receive anything from the Lord" (James 1:7-8).

When we doubt and worry, our hearts become divided. Even momentary disbelief stirs up fears. Being of two minds, we become anxious and can't fulfill the will of God.

God works in the lives of those who have faith in him. Holiness comes when we trust everything to him. We should be single-minded, devoted to God in both mind and heart.

God doesn't delight in confusion. When things become jumbled and confused, our holiness breaks down. In the book of Leviticus God gives the Israelites many instructions about how to organize their lives and possessions. He forbids planting two different kinds of seeds in the same field; he warns against mixing certain fabrics in clothes (Leviticus 19:19).

The Old Testament prohibits animals of different species from mating (Leviticus 19:19). It dictates that cows and donkeys shouldn't be yoked together at the plow (Deuteronomy

22:10). It also warns about drinking wine:

> Who has woe? Who has sorrow?
>   Who has strife? Who has complaining?
> Who has wounds without cause?
>   Who has redness of eyes?
> Those who linger late over wine,
>   those who keep trying mixed wines. (Proverbs 23:29-30)

God is against double-mindedness, divided loyalties, in every aspect of the spiritual life. He forbids idol worship. He forbids adultery. Paul takes up the cry: "Do you not know that whoever is united to a prostitute becomes one body with her? For it is said, 'The two shall be one flesh.' But anyone united to the Lord becomes one spirit with him" (1 Corinthians 6:16-17).

To live a life with one purpose we must make decisions every minute of every day. A good example occurs in the book of Daniel. When Daniel was held captive he found that the meat and wine provided by the king weren't appropriate for an Israelite. He asked the palace master if he could have vegetables and water instead. And so he was served, with the result that Daniel and his friends thrived (Daniel 1:8-15).

But Daniel's troubles were not over. "The presidents and the satraps tried to find grounds for complaint against [him] in connection with the kingdom. But they could find no grounds for complaint or any corruption, because he was faithful, and no negligence or corruption could be found in him" (Daniel 6:4).

Such was Daniel's remarkable life. And such must be our lives. What's the secret of having such a heart for God? Knowing the glory God has in store. We must decide to please God only. We need to have a heart for God.

41

Influencing Others
Through Righteousness

❧

One reason we seek the discipline of holiness is for its influence on others. Consider those in church history who are known as saints. We don't so much revere them for their great achievements as for their spiritual attitudes. What stands out in their lives is their motives for living, to love God and to care for lost souls. And their influence on others was remarkable.

Look at Jesus! Jesus didn't become a recognized author or celebrity. He didn't found a mission organization or build great skyscrapers. He wasn't a world traveler. But his influence transcends his generation, ethnicity, country of origin.

The influence of Jesus is timeless and eternal. Grounded in holiness, he overturns the common view that wealth, political power, sexual dominance and high learning have the greatest impact. Instead, he shows us that lowliness and holiness and spiritual blessing are what really move the world.

One shining example of this kind of holiness is Robert Murray McCheyne who was summoned by God at a very young age. According to his biographer William MacDonald, in *Be Holy,* Mc-

Cheyne's holiness was noticeable even before he spoke a word; his appearance and manner spoke for him. People just sensed the presence of God in him and believed that he was God's messenger. Yes, holiness was the source of his powerful influence.

His biographer tells this story about him: "There was a minister in the North of Scotland with whom he spent the night. He was so marvelously struck by this about him that when Mr. McCheyne left the room, he burst into tears and said, 'Oh, that is the most Jesus-like man I ever saw.' "

His biographer went on to analyze his intense holiness.

> McCheyne spent hours in holy communion inside the Veil, in rapturous praise and adoration, being bathed in Calvary's Love. He would come forth from God's presence to leave the fragrance of Christ as he went from house to house in visitation. As he walked the streets of his parish—and even anywhere in Britain—the people were startled to see the look of Jesus upon his face.

The Bible sets a high value on holiness. According to Genesis, Sodom and Gomorrah didn't have ten righteous people and had to pay the ultimate price (Genesis 18:32). According to Jeremiah God promised he would pardon Jerusalem if there was one righteous person there (Jeremiah 5:1). According to Paul the sin of one man, Adam, brought death to all humanity (Romans 5:12).

Because of one person, Jesus, the door to salvation opened wide (Romans 5:17). When just one person in Egypt, Joseph, was persevering in faith, Egypt and other countries experienced deliverance. When one person, Moses, had his hands lifted up, the Israelites won battles against the Amalekites.

God is looking for just one person who hates sin, fears God and is willing to lay his or her life aside to fulfill God's mission. He's looking for those who will make holiness their highest goal. Because of one righteous person, a blessing will come to our own place and time.

Such a blessing came through Daniel to the country where he lived, and through Paul to open the door of salvation to the world.

Yes, God wants to find those who aren't seeking popularity and fame but are looking for genuine holiness, and we are the ones.

We are the ones he expects to grow in holy discipline to influence the world.

42

Our Goal
in Righteousness

The righteousness of the servants of God has the power to influence others. It also transcends time and place. But, sad to say, this righteous influence can be corrupted by sin.

Righteousness has power, yes, but evil isn't without its own power and influence. Sin can destroy whatever it touches, bringing on curses, judgments and dissension. Once sin enters into a righteous person, it cripples him or her spiritually.

Make no mistake! Sin isn't a concept. It's a living organism. It destroyed the Garden of Eden. It ruins individuals, families, communities, even nations. But, glad to say, righteousness can restore them all.

Whenever righteousness touches sinful nature, great repentance will take place. An unworthy person, confronted by righteousness, may be drawn into godliness and transformed.

All things became new when Jesus came into the world. By this time the descendants of Adam had a sinful nature embedded in them, but that nature was made new again when Jesus touched them (2 Corinthians 5:17).

Read the Gospels with a discerning spirit, and you'll see this influence. What happened to the places Jesus visited? How did he transform the ones he met? What about the families who offered him hospitality? Overcoming original sin, he restored them.

Wherever Jesus visited, repentance was felt and transformation took place. The Samaritan woman, tax collectors and the chief tax collector Zacchaeus—all experienced conversion. The righteous hands of our Lord Jesus changed everything.

We too seek for holy living because we believe in the power of righteousness. But what is the meaning of righteous living? What is its goal? The goal of righteousness is none other than Jesus. Those who long for righteousness imitate Jesus.

The story is told in *Be Holy* (by William MacDonald) of Sandu Singh, a Hindu who was a convert to Christianity. He visited a home and was greeted by a maid; upon seeing him she shouted to her master that Jesus had come.

In another incident he prayed for little children; they were so deeply touched by his presence that they told their mother, "We want to have Jesus come and sleep with us."

His biographer explained it this way. "All these things are simply expressions of [those] who met him. Life that resembled Jesus with meekness harmonized with his authority splendidly manifested."

Yes, Jesus is the goal for all believers.

No doubt it's very important to have responsibility in a church. Yet when we stand before God, we'll soon find out that our titles in the churches aren't so important. The only thing God looks for is how much we have become like Jesus. According to McCheyne, there's no more important skill than imitating Jesus Christ. Our ultimate goal is to become like Christ.

Let us ardently desire righteousness.

Let us show the face of Jesus to others.

Let us be righteous tools of God who restores our nature from a life shattered and broken by sin.

43

Discipline in Righteousness
Is Life Long

The deadliest disease of contemporary life is impatience. Quoting a remark by psychiatrist Carl Jung, Richard Foster points out in *Celebration of Discipline* that "hurry is not *of* the devil, it *is* the devil." People would rather have a quick success than a gradual one. They boast about overnight success. But there's one thing we can't achieve overnight: the discipline of righteousness.

God disciplines his servants thoroughly to ready them for the ministry. But such preparation takes a long time; it doesn't happen overnight.

Consider Joseph, son of Jacob. He seemed flawless, but God put him through thirteen years as a slave and prisoner to purge away the invisible flaws from his life, like dross from gold.

Consider Moses. God kept him in desert training for forty years. Even Joshua had to train as a subordinate to him during those years.

Adam, the first human, was holy from birth, but he wasn't mature; he fell so easily into Satan's temptation and disobeyed God. But God took into account the deficiencies of his life, a life without stages of growth. He saw to it that the new Adam, Jesus, began as an infant. As Jesus grew older he also grew wiser. Not until he was thirty years old did he finish his preparation.

Jesus learned obedience through suffering (Hebrews 5:8), and even then it wasn't over. The first Adam didn't go through such trials, but Jesus (the second Adam) was thoroughly prepared by trials of the soul. Once Jesus was equipped in righteousness, he was able to resist Satan and obeyed God even to death.

The first king of Israel, Saul, became a king a without any preparation. His immature character, so unsuited for kingly responsibilities, eventually turned his life into a disaster. For this reason God made sure that his second king wouldn't follow a similar path.

Consider David. From his young days as a shepherd to his time of kingship at age thirty he had to flee from Saul, living in caves and wilderness to prepare for the future. Even on the day when this young man was anointed ruler, trials were already waiting for him.

Once God decides to give a person greater ministry, he allots preparation time. Think of how plants flourish in the natural world. Some mushrooms spring up in just six hours; squash takes six months. An ordinary oak tree needs six years, but a full, spreading oak tree takes a hundred years.

We need to decide what kind of servants of God we want to be! To be like the great oak tree, we shouldn't be impatient. "I am confident of this," wrote Paul, "that the one who began a good work among you will bring it to completion by the day of Jesus Christ" (Philippians 1:6). Paul understood that our righteousness will be truly complete at the day of Jesus Christ.

Is righteousness a gift, or must we cultivate it? Righteousness comes as part of the gift of faith—when we first believe in Jesus. But to complete that righteousness is a lifelong process. God did not give us a short cut.

God first puts a desire in us about righteousness (Philippians 2:13). Only God can make us righteous, but he will not complete that righteousness without our will and dedication. To bring it to completion, we must cooperate with God's grace.

Let us consider the life of Jesus. Daily he prayed and meditated on the Word. We should follow his example.

PART EIGHT

The Way of Transformation

44

See Your True Identity

Spiritual formation begins the day we meet Jesus. That day we begin to understand our true identities. First, we get a glimpse of our ugly side. Second, we discover our splendid, unlimited potential. Such a vision of our true nature is one of the great gifts God gives us.

Here is what Isaiah said when he met God: "I am lost, for I am a man of unclean lips, and I live among a people of unclean lips; yet my eyes have seen the King, the LORD of hosts" (Isaiah 6:5)! Yes, it was only after he met God that he began to understand his own unworthiness.

Something similar happened to Peter. Jesus told him that if he wanted to catch fish that day, he should cast his net in deep water, not in shallow. So Peter did what he was told and hauled in a huge load of fish. Then he fell down at Jesus' knees. "Go away from me, Lord, for I am a sinful man!" (Luke 5:8). Yes, he could have said thanks, but instead he felt he had to confess his sin.

Those with deep spirituality have a strong conviction about their sinful natures. Abraham is a good example: "I am nothing but dust and ashes" (Genesis 18:27 NIV)—that's how he described himself when he prayed for Sodom and Gomorrah.

Paul claimed to be "foremost" among sinners (1 Timothy 1:15) and referred to himself as "one untimely born" (1 Corinthians 15:8). In his case, the closer he got to God, the closer he got to himself.

The closer we get to God, the clearer our sight becomes. The Lord said, "Blessed are the pure in heart, for they will see God" (Matthew 5:8). Yes, we'll see God, but only after we are aware of our sins, fear our failures, see how wicked we have become.

Think of a person trying to tidy up a garden. Some gardeners notice only the large rocks. But when they put on their glasses, they can see the small.

Spiritual sight works the same way. With vision blurred by original sin we can deal only with our gross sinful nature. But a person who has a deep spiritual life easily sees even the smaller sins and imperfections.

Sometimes, as we grow in grace, we get the feeling that we're growing in sin. When this happens we shouldn't yell to high heaven; we should give thanks. We should be grateful that God has saved us and called us to a righteous life. Now we understand Paul when he says to the Romans, "where sin increased, grace abounded all the more" (Romans 5:20).

What a contrast between our sinful nature and the grace of God! Our dedication should continue to grow, fueled not so much by regret for sin as by appreciation of grace.

45

The Guidance of Patience

※

How can we measure a person's spiritual maturity? Paul tells us how: "The signs of a true apostle were performed among you with utmost patience" (2 Corinthians 12:12).

When Paul wrote to his spiritual son Timothy, he called himself the lowest of the low. "I received mercy, so that in me, as the foremost, Christ might display the utmost patience, making me an example to those who would come to believe in him for eternal life" (1 Timothy 1:16). Later in the same letter, he emphasized the importance of perseverance.

First and Second Timothy are pastoral letters, encouraging pastors to give more importance to patience. "If we endure, we will also reign with him; if we deny him, he will also deny us" (2 Timothy 2:12).

Paul instructed his friend as a minister of God. "The Lord's servant must not be quarrelsome but kindly to everyone, an apt teacher, patient, correcting opponents with gentleness" (2 Timothy 2:24-25).

Those who engage in teaching and preaching the gospel need to have endurance. Paul emphasized this over and over. "Proclaim the message; be persistent whether the time is favorable or unfavorable; convince, rebuke, and encourage, with the utmost patience in teaching" (2 Timothy 4:2).

Why is patience so important? Patience is the essence of love. Love is what God expects to find in his servants. Love allows God's servants to endure. A person with patience is a loving person, and a person with love is a persevering person.

In a famous description Paul defined love from first to last: "Love is patient. . . . [It] endures all things" (1 Corinthians 13:4, 7). The first word, *patient*, concerns the way we treat other human beings. The last word, *endures* (also translated as *perseveres*), is about dealing with the life we are living, coping with our own nature.

Though we accept persons as they are, we also expect them to change for the better. True patience hopes for the better and envisions the best. This "envisioning" is full of love and also full of power. Think of Joseph, who was able to persevere against temptation with the help of his visions and dreams.

Jesus also had a vision of the world's salvation. That vision of his, closely linked to patience, helped him resist temptation.

After feeding the five thousand, Jesus was able to resist the people who wanted to make him a king. Endurance also helped him to withstand the punishment of the cross. Yet he was able to endure the cross because he saw the vision of the resurrection and glory.

> Let us run with perseverance the race that is set before us, looking to Jesus the pioneer and perfecter of our faith, who for the sake of the joy that was set before him endured the cross, disregarding its shame, and has taken his seat at the right hand of the throne of God. (Hebrews12:1-2)

Let endurance have its full effect, so that you may be mature and complete, lacking in nothing. (James 1:4)

For those who want to engage in deeper spiritual disciplines, patience is a prerequisite. Patience is a sign of spiritual maturity. People who have patience lack nothing. People who have patience have everything.

Let's have patience. Let's think about Jesus and endure.

46

Discovering Self-Control

Self-control is the height of spiritual discipline. It's the ninth and last spiritual fruit mentioned in Galatians (5:22). Assisting in the cultivation of self-control is the Holy Spirit.

"Before we can conquer the world, we must first conquer the self," wrote Oswald Sanders in *Spiritual Leadership.* In other words, it's one thing to get the better of someone else, but by far the more difficult thing is getting the better of oneself.

"Mastering others requires force," wrote Lao Tzu in *Tao Te Ching,* "mastering the self needs strength." Those who can tame themselves are valiant soldiers in the battle against self. It's the battle of a lifetime. We have to conquer or be conquered. It's a battle to the death.

To master ourselves, we must first know ourselves. "Knowing others is wisdom," writes Lao Tzu; "knowing the self is enlightenment." How can we come to know ourselves? By practicing the disciplines, but even then we'll know ourselves in part. Only when we come before God will we know who we really are.

Isaiah saw his ugly nature when he met God. Peter confessed that he was a sinner after an encounter with Jesus. We must find God in the words of the Word in order to know who we are. The

Word reflects our image like a mirror. These mirror images come from God, and we need God to know ourselves.

Where does the power of self-control come from?

First, it comes through the Holy Spirit. Our own strength, as we well know, has its limits. As Jesus said to his disciples, "the spirit indeed is willing, but the flesh is weak" (Matthew 26:41). But when they received the power of the Holy Spirit, things changed. Then they had strength to overcome their weaknesses. Hence, we too should look for the power of the Holy Spirit in our own lives.

Second, self-control comes about through all the spiritual disciplines. They strengthen us. They help us to acquire holy habits. They make soldiers of us in the perpetual battle against self.

Athletes have their own exercise programs. They continually try to improve their performance. Like the rest of us, they also tend to slack off. Unlike the rest of us, they exercise so much in their lives that they acquire massive self-control, at least in the physical life. We would do well to emulate their blood, sweat and tears in the spiritual realm.

47

Skill in Language

✦

"All of us make many mistakes," we find in the book of James. "Anyone who makes no mistakes in speaking is perfect, able to keep the whole body in check with a bridle" (James 3:2). No wonder spiritually mature people have power.

Jesus possessed the word power to move human souls. I've pondered his words for a long time, and this is what I found: Two disciples on the way to Emmaus spoke about things that had recently taken place. When Jesus asked them what, they replied, "The things about Jesus of Nazareth, who was a prophet mighty in deed and word before God and all the people" (Luke 24:19).

Yes, as we know from Luke and the other evangelists, Jesus had verbal gifts. His words spoke to the people. His words revealed his own spirituality. Looking back through the New Testament, we find in him a harmony of language, character and ministry.

"I have not spoken on my own, but the Father who sent me has himself given me a commandment about what to say and what to speak" (John 12:49). Yes, God the Father showed his Son how to speak, what to say, when to begin speaking, when to stop. In these, as well as other things, Jesus was always guided by his Father.

Once we are filled with the Holy Spirit our language will change.

The Holy Spirit will teach us what we need to know. No longer will we have to worry about what to say. Jesus taught his disciples, "it is not you who speak, but the Spirit of your Father speaking through you" (Matthew 10:20).

The Holy Spirit brought the church into being, empowering those who were present with many languages: "All of them were filled with the Holy Spirit and began to speak in other languages, as the Spirit gave them ability" (Acts 2:4).

Stephen was outstanding among the deacons of the early church in spiritual discipline. Luke describes him this way: "They could not withstand the wisdom and the Spirit with which he spoke" (Acts 6:10).

To be mature in the use of language, we must first master our inner world. Whatever fills our hearts will overflow and make itself known. "We cannot keep from speaking about what we have seen and heard" (Acts 4:20).

Jesus put it this way: "You brood of vipers! How can you speak good things, when you are evil? For out of the abundance of the heart the mouth speaks. The good person brings good things out of a good treasure, and the evil person brings evil things out of an evil treasure" (Matthew 12:34-35).

To fill our hearts with good things we must be careful what we read, see and hear. We should choose friends wisely. We should select those who will have a good influence on us. Paul sounded a warning: "Do not be deceived: 'Bad company ruins good morals' " (1 Corinthians 15:33).

To perfect our language we must practice the discipline of solitude. Solitude keeps a tight rein on our tongues. "Be silent," says the ancient Greek philosopher Pythagoras. "Break the silence only if you have something better to say."

As we suspect, silence isn't the only answer. We need to discern when silence is needed. Once again Paul issues a warning: "Let your speech always be gracious, seasoned with salt, so that you may know how you ought to answer everyone" (Colossians 4:6). What Paul means is that our conversation should be gracious. When we balance silence and expression, encouragement and rebuke, then we're acting as mature Christians.

48

Satisfied in Spirit

✤

What distinguishes mature servants of God? They're content with what they have. David said, "my cup overflows" (Psalm 23:5). He served the Lord as his shepherd and experienced that generous overflow. His contentment didn't arise from being a king, having great wealth or winning victory in battle; it came from God.

Paul was also content with what he had. "Not that I am referring to being in need," he wrote, "for I have learned to be content with whatever I have. I know what it is to have little, and I know what it is to have plenty. In any and all circumstances I have learned the secret of being well-fed and of going hungry, of having plenty and of being in need" (Philippians 4:11-12). Only after coming to know Jesus did Paul learn the secret of contentment.

Those who are born in original sin are never content with their situations. Human greed is limitless. What did Adam and Eve crave in the Garden of Eden? They wanted the one thing that God forbade them to eat, the fruit of the tree of knowledge of good and evil.

We too want to be like gods. Humanity's greed is unlimited; no matter what we have, still we're not satisfied. Proverbs, written so many centuries ago, records our insatiable desire. "Sheol and

Abaddon are never satisfied, / and human eyes are never satisfied"
(Proverbs 27:20). Again from Proverbs:

> The leech has two daughters;
>   "Give! Give!" they cry.
> Three things are never satisfied;
>   four never say, "Enough":
> Sheol, the barren womb,
>   the earth ever thirsty for water,
>   and the fire that never says, "Enough." (Proverbs 30:15-16)

If we are dissatisfied with those around us, then our lives aren't
filled to the brim. But what can fill our lives to overflowing? True
satisfaction is only possible when we fill our lives not with worldly
things but with the precious Lord. When the Lord who is greater
than the world comes into our hearts, satisfaction will overwhelm
us. "In him all the fullness of God was pleased to dwell" (Colossians 1:19).

Jesus is the one who fills the whole world (Ephesians 1:23). For
this reason, those who have been seized by the love of Jesus will be
content with what they have.

The Bible mentions two things that are unending, the appetite
of human beings and the love of God. But we have ways to deal
with this insatiable greed of ours. We must experience the bound-
less love of God. That's when human beings will learn all about
contentment.

Many Christians, however, aren't happy with their lives because
they look for satisfaction apart from Jesus. They're entranced by
the things of the world. John Oppenheim, quoted by Zig Zigler in
Steps to the Top, once said, "The foolish man seeks happiness in the
distance; the wise man grows it under his feet."

Believers don't have to look far for happiness; they find it in Jesus who makes his home right here with us. Let's gaze on him, the source of all satisfaction. Let's avoid difficult situations, complex human relationships and worldly anxieties, things that try to ruin our contentment. Let's live with Jesus and be content.

49

Have a Heart Like Jesus

One of our most difficult spiritual challenges has to do with opening our hearts; embracing others in our hearts. How can we deal with this? Only by the grace of God.

Here's an example from the Bible: "God gave Solomon very great wisdom, discernment, and breadth of understanding as vast as the sand on the seashore" (1 Kings 4:29). God made Solomon wise, yes, but he also changed his heart.

Some people seem to have been born with generous hearts; this is a gift of grace. But don't consider this a matter of fate. Our hearts can be changed. Paul promised that to the believers in Corinth. "There is no restriction in our affections, but only in yours. In return—I speak as to children—open wide your hearts also" (2 Corinthians 6:12-13). These verses are encouraging.

How can we tell the difference between a generous and an ungenerous heart?

First, by the way a person treats others. As Fred Smith has said in his book *Learning to Lead*, "Immature individuals can't enjoy people who are different. They prefer people just like themselves. Maturity is being comfortable with diversity."

Second, by noticing how others react to us. When we toss a rock into the pool at the base of a small fountain, the ripples run riot. Toss that same rock into a large lake, and it will make lovely circular ripples. In a small pot, water boils in no time; in a large kettle, water takes its time in coming to a boil. Think about it. How quickly do our personalities come to a boil? Too quickly is the answer. Our anger, or quick temper, reveals that we aren't the persons we want to be.

Sometimes when people think differently from us, we're quick to say they're wrong. But being different isn't necessarily wrong. There are differences among people, and mature people appreciate them; they even learn from them. As we expand our hearts to embrace others, we'll accept, understand and love their differences.

Those who refuse to embrace others are thinking only about themselves. They don't care much about the other person's happiness. *What's in it for me?* they're thinking. When they don't stand to gain, they fly off the handle.

So, how can we open our hearts to embrace others? Only by having a heart like Jesus who embraced the whole world. Even when he was threatened, he didn't lose his temper. Paul behaved in much the same way.

How do true servants of God behave? They don't put themselves first. They're guided entirely by the Word of God. For the sake of the gospel, they embrace everyone; they open their hearts to receive one and all.

Let's have a heart like Jesus. Let's open our hearts to embrace everyone!

50

Embracing One and All

🌿

Let the same mind be in you that was in Christ Jesus" (Philippians 2:5). What did Paul mean when he said that? What did Jesus mean when he said, "Take my yoke upon you, and learn from me; for I am gentle and humble in heart, and you will find rest for your souls" (Matthew 11:29)? Yes, the heart of Jesus is gentle and humble. Yes, when he reigns in us, we'll have true rest.

The heart of Jesus is meek. It embraces everyone. It's comfortable but durable; it's smooth as silk and yet hard as steel.

A meek heart is also a warm heart. Warmth is a sign of life. Little children feel warm to our touch. Healthy people glow with warmth. As we near the end of life, we begin to lose our warmth and indeed our health; we feel the cold more and more.

The same thing holds true with a community. A vibrant community has warmth and tenderness. It's flexible, gracious and has a heart to embrace everyone. A dying community, on the other hand, is cold, hard and stiff; it suffers from tensions, overinterprets the laws and sets up barriers between people.

People want to embrace—and be embraced by—a person with a meek heart. For them such an embrace can be transforming. It's something like the warm embrace that allows a baby chick to hatch: a nurturing environment. An eggshell cracks, and the young chick appears.

The meek heart of Jesus embraces everyone: tax collectors, prostitutes, sinners, the poor, the wealthy, the ignorant and the intelligent. They are transformed by this warm embrace. People who have been hard-shelled as eggs can experience renewal. With Jesus, their shells break. They come eagerly into the world. As we grow deeper in spiritual disciplines, we will no longer criticize, discriminate and condemn. Like Jesus, we'll embrace everyone.

The heart of Jesus is a humble heart. It ascends to high places and descends to low places. It's always at home, no matter what the neighborhood, although it seems more at home with the lowly than the mighty.

Consider the great earth! It receives everything at its lowest elevation. It gathers all living things. It can reproduce life. The earth receives rubbish, falling leaves, seeds from farmers and even from fruit trees. Then it transforms whatever it has received, giving back life in the form of beautiful flowers and blessed fruit. It is no great stretch of the imagination to compare Jesus with an earth like this.

Take a look at the ocean! An ocean is lower than any rivers that flow into it. An ocean receives clean things and dirty things, fair things and foul, and then transforms them all. The ocean accepts everything.

Jesus is also like an ocean. From the lowliest elevation he embraces everyone. When we speak about deeper spirituality, both earth and ocean are good comparisons. They embrace everything; in the same way, we should embrace everyone.

51

Uncomfortable and Abundant

Jesus didn't promise a comfortable life, but he did promise an abundant life. What's the difference? "The thief comes only to steal and kill and destroy," John quotes Jesus as saying. "I come that they may have life, and have it abundantly" (John 10:10).

The abundant life Jesus was talking about is the happy life. It's not the comfortable life. It's the life filled with spiritual meaning and worthwhile tasks.

Jesus is the model of what abundance and happiness are all about. When he chose to abandon heaven, he forfeited comfort. He was born in a manger, fled to Egypt, grew up in Nazareth. To those who wanted to follow him he said, "Foxes have holes, and birds of the air have nests; but the Son of Man has nowhere to lay his head" (Luke 9:58).

Jesus had little time for himself while he lived in this world; he spent most of his time helping those who needed him. But all the time he was filled with joy. He enjoyed saving others, healing others, loving others. He filled his own life by giving himself away to others.

One day I found myself meditating on those who receive callings from God. The one thing they had in common was that they all left their comfortable homes behind. Some had going-away parties given by friends and relatives; others simply found themselves left out in the cold, like the eaglets who have been dumped from their warm and cozy nests by their mother. Sometimes God dumps us from our nests.

When God called Abraham to leave his home in Ur, the patriarch hit the road with nowhere to go. When God showed dreams to Joseph, the young man was faced with the life of a slave and a prisoner. When David was anointed king by Samuel, he became a fugitive from Saul.

When Jesus called the disciples, they had to abandon their fathers and boats to follow him; all of them except John faced uncomfortable death by martyrdom. When Paul received a calling on the road to Damascus, suffering was waiting in his immediate future (Acts 9:15-16). All these servants of God lived uncomfortable lives, but they gained the abundant life, the happy life, by fulfilling the will of God.

An uncomfortable life isn't necessarily a miserable life. On the other hand, a comfortable life doesn't guarantee a happy life. A good example is Nehemiah. He believed that an uncomfortable life was a blessing. While in the palace of Susa, he heard about the ruin of Jerusalem and wept. Then he voiced this prayer: "Give success to your servant today" (Nehemiah 1:11). Then he gave up his comfortable life in the palace and lived a painful life in Jerusalem, rebuilding the wall. Though it was uncomfortable, he believed that it is a blessing to do the will of God.

Human happiness is found in the abundant life. The abundant life comes when we live a life of mission (Acts 20:24); a life that serves others has meaning and purpose (Mark 10:45). It's the content of a life that counts, not the length of it.

When evaluating your life, don't be confused by length of it or the fast pace of it! Rather, reflect on the content of life.

Put aside the comfortable life, and decide on the abundant life.

The uncomfortable life is where God wants us to be (Matthew 7:13-14).

52

The Way of Transformation

Attaining spiritual maturity isn't easy. Relentless training is needed, much like the training Paul took on when he became obedient to God. Such training requires sacrifice: you must despise sin, be passionate for holiness and balance your work with mature living. Not only that; spiritual maturity shouldn't be the goal in itself. Instead, our goal should be to witness truly to Jesus in our lives. When all is said and done our spiritual maturity must be for the sake of ministry.

True meaning and purpose are lost when a person focuses entirely on gaining spiritual maturity. But beware. Mature spirituality is no substitute for ministry. And heads up! If one boasts about having achieved spiritual maturity, then that person has to start all over again. That's not what spirituality is all about.

Gaining spiritual maturity is hard; losing it is easy. On this very subject Paul sent this warning to the Corinthians: "So if you think you are standing, watch out that you do not fall" (1 Corinthians 10:12).

Satan is busily tempting us throughout our lives. His strategies take on many different forms. We already know this, but we need to be aware and stay on guard. We know from experience that as temptations begin, so they end; they don't last forever. That was the experience of Jesus; that was what Luke put in his Gospel. "When the devil had finished every test, he departed from him" (Luke 4:13).

What then is the prescription for maintaining exceptional spirituality?

First, we must learn to walk the straight path. That's what God told Joshua: "Do not turn from it to the right hand or to the left, that you may be successful wherever you go" (Joshua 1:7). Walk straight ahead, don't be diverted this way or that. Proverbs teaches the following: "Hear, my child, and be wise, / and direct your mind in the way" (Proverbs 23:19).

Jesus also has some travel directions: "Enter through the narrow gate; for the gate is wide and the road is easy that leads to destruction, and there are many who take it. For the gate is narrow and the road is hard that leads to life, and there are few who find it" (Matthew 7:13-14). The people of God often must take the difficult path, not the easy one. We must choose the narrow road: the road of the cross.

Second, we must abide in Jesus always. Our goal must always be Christ. Apart from Jesus we can't and shouldn't do anything. As Paul said, we must not lean on what we see, or fall into the snares of materialism. Nor should we be caught up in legalism in the name of spiritual training. Impossible demands of worship, self-demeaning practices, severity to the body—none of these should be considered a spiritual goal (Colossians 2:19, 21-23). We must always be connected to Christ, who is the head of the body. We must abide in (John 15:5), contemplate (Hebrews 3:1) and gaze at (Hebrews 12:2) Jesus, the object of our faith.

Third, we must live a Spirit-filled life (Ephesians 5:18).

To live a Christlike life without the help of the Holy Spirit is impossible.

We can become like Jesus only by relying on the Spirit Jesus sends us (2 Corinthians 3:18). The Spirit of Jesus frees us. When we're training in the Spirit we dance with freedom and joy. When we follow in the Spirit we won't give way to the desires of the flesh (Galatians 5:16). The Spirit-filled life is also a Word-filled life. The Word of Jesus is Spirit and life (John 6:63).

Fourth, to follow Jesus we must deny ourselves daily. Jesus spoke to those who wanted to be his disciples: "If any want to become my followers, let them deny themselves and take up their cross daily and follow me" (Luke 9:23). The operative word here is *daily*. To follow the way of Jesus is to deny oneself daily. Paul also says, "I die every day!" (1 Corinthians 15:31). Paul's exceptional spiritual maturity comes from "dying daily." We know if we neglect our gardens for even a day, weeds will appear again. Our minds and bodies are the same way. We can't afford to neglect our spiritual training.

Fifth, to do battle against Satan, we must try to be always awake and on guard. The apostle Peter reminds us: "Discipline yourselves, keep alert. Like a roaring lion your adversary the devil prowls around looking for someone to devour" (1 Peter 5:8). Remember, Peter had been tripped up by Satan when he denied Jesus three times during Jesus' final hours. That's why Peter urged us to be alert. He knew he wasn't above temptation.

Paul knew this too. He urged us to be ready by putting on the full armor of God (Ephesians 6:10-17). The only way to be victorious is to be constantly, relentlessly praying in the Spirit.

Sixth, our love of God in Jesus compels us to serve others. Jesus summed up the commandments in one simple statement, that we should love God and love our neighbor (Matthew 22:37-40). One sign of being a disciple of Christ is demonstrating his love (John 13:34-35). Paul went as far as to say that without love all our actions will count as nothing (1 Corinthians 13:1-3). Knowledge, wisdom, understanding and even the deepest spirituality mean nothing without love. Only by love can we be patient and endure all things.

Last, our ministry calls for a balance in spirituality and the Word. We must empty ourselves of our sinful nature to be filled with the powerful Word of God. We must also spread the Word that we are filled with; then we should empty ourselves again to be filled even more abundantly. Only then will we know spirituality in its fullness.

Once again I would like to stress that balance is the most important thing in mature spirituality. Ministry is valid only when it flows out of a close relationship with Jesus and imitation of him. True spirituality is the work of a ministry that comes out of a person's mature character.

The early church achieved a great ministry of world evangelism—but not by good or perfect character. Even though they were transformed by Jesus, the disciples were by no means perfect; on the contrary, they were quite imperfect. Their great work of the ministry came from the power of the Holy Spirit and was constantly under trial.

Good and mature character, however, is a vessel in which the Holy Spirit works mightily, and a foundation on which the ministry can be built. Because human character is so limited, we must always trust and lean on the working of the Holy Spirit, the blood of Jesus and his righteousness. We must attend to the work of the ministry in the power and authority of Jesus' name.

How shall we describe the life of a Christlike person? Such a life sets a goal and imitates Jesus in a lifelong process by and in the grace of God. Paul set only one life goal, and that was to be like Jesus. Paul imitated Jesus throughout his life, but still confessed, "Beloved, I do not consider that I have made it on my own; but this one thing I do: forgetting what lies behind and straining forward to what lies ahead, I press on toward the goal for the prize of the heavenly call of God in Christ Jesus" (Philippians 3:13-14). Paul dedicated his life to Christ's call, but he felt that he had to make a confession: "I do not count my life of any value to myself, if only I may finish my course and the ministry that I received from the Lord Jesus, to testify to the good news of God's grace" (Acts 20:24).

Afterword

❧

I first heard Pastor Joshua Choonmin Kang at the Renovaré Covenant Retreat in Estes Park, Colorado, in the summer of 2004.

Everyone there was struck by his simplicity and depth as he led us through reflections and meditations on John 15.

These talks were given over three days. He spoke in English in the morning, and gave a comparable message in Korean in the afternoon, with Pastor Brian Kang interpreting. Brian Kang also spoke at the retreat, which was led by Richard Foster.

At some point the question of language became paramount. "Christ is a language," said Pastor Joshua Kang. Ethnic difference may divide us, but Jesus Christ unifies us. Most of us at the retreat were English-speaking people, but not all of us were from the United States; we represented many localities, several nations. All were touched by his words. They had the ring of Paul to the Galatians. "There is no longer Jew nor Greek, there is no longer slave or free, there is no longer male and female; for all of you are one in Christ Jesus" (Galatians 3:28).

Several months later my husband and I went to visit Pastor

Joshua Kang at his church in Los Angeles, presenting ourselves at the Oriental Mission Church as candidates to help edit this book. We attended the early morning (5:20 a.m.) prayer service.

The church was nearly filled—it holds about a thousand people—and the atmosphere was hushed. The service was in Korean, of which we speak not a word, but we could feel the intensity of the congregation. At certain moments the prayer was spontaneous. Hands were lifted. People spoke to Jesus.

Christ is a language, I found myself thinking. We were praying too. On the lectern used by Pastor Kang I noticed the Greek letters Alpha and Omega. Somehow the Spirit was leaping over the barriers of race and ethnicity.

My husband, William Griffin, and I have served as editors of *Deep-Rooted in Christ: The Way of Transformation.* Our aim was to let Pastor Joshua Kang speak for himself in his own distinctive voice. As we worked, we remained faithful to his Asian way of thinking, his rural and agricultural and seafaring metaphors, so reminiscent of the teaching style Jesus himself used. We were struck by the biblical depth, the rootedness of his writing.

Western readers will be blessed by this book. The thought and writing are simple and fresh. Pastor Joshua Choonmin Kang brings his own insight and gentle spirit to Christian life. His work will regenerate and enliven us as he teaches us how to become "deep people."

Emilie Griffin

Acknowledgments

This book exists thanks to the prayer and support of many people.

I would like to thank Pastor Brian Kang, Pastor Doug Spriggs and Pastor Byoung-Chul Jun for the translation work; Emilie Griffin and William Griffin for their editing work; and Cindy Bunch for her shepherding this book to publication.

My special and very deep thanks goes to Richard J. Foster for his writing the foreword; he is a God-appointed spiritual leader for his own generation. Many of his spiritual sayings and teachings are reflected in my own writings. Without his encouragement this book would have not been published in English.

I also wish to thank those who prayed for me until this book was published: my mother, my wife Grace, my daughters Rebekah and Esther, and my pastoral staff.

Most of all, I give my thanks to Jesus who led me deep into his spiritual world.